Introduction

The English Coordination Group has been set up with the aim of producing specialised revision material for National Curriculum English. This book provides concise coverage of the Key Stage Four syllabus for _GCSE English_ up to Higher Level with particular emphasis on essential Grammar, Spelling and Punctuation.

Our Guides have _three features_ which set them apart from the rest:

Careful and Concise Explanations and Rules

We work hard to give accurate, concise and carefully written details on each topic. This guide places particular emphasis on learning Thirty Rules to improve Grammar, Spelling and Punctuation — areas where students frequently lose valuable marks.

Deliberate Use of Humour

We consider the humour to be an essential part of our Revision Guides. It's there to keep the reader interested and entertained, and we are certain that it greatly assists their learning. We don't expect to win any awards for it though...

Provision of Models for Critical Reading and Writing

This guide offers a range of simplified models to introduce the key skills and techniques of literary criticism for fiction and non-fiction texts. These techniques include comprehension, critical reading, essay writing and personal writing skills. We also give practical advice on reading and writing about different styles of text — focusing on language, tone, bias and context.

Contents

Essential English

Reading Skills

Writing Skills

Examples and Reference

Published by Coordination Group Publications
Typesetting, layout and illustrations by The English Coordination Group
Original illustrations by: Sandy Gardner, e-mail: Zimkit@aol.com

Written and Edited by Simon Cook BA (Hons)
Design Editor: James Paul Wallis BEng (Hons)

Contributions by:
Anne Alexander, Hayley Croser, Frances Cross, Paul Sabbage, Caroline Toms, Marjorie Willetts

Clipart Source: CorelDRAW

Printed by Hindson Print, Newcastle upon Tyne.

Learning the Rules

This book is about how to pick up _good marks_ for GCSE English or English Literature. This first Section will tell you what you can do to _improve_ your _work_ — and improve your _marks_ too.

You Need Two Skills to Improve Your Marks

1) _Make sure_ you _don't_ make any _mistakes_ in your _grammar_, _spelling_ or _punctuation_.
2) _Practise_ writing _clearly_ and _accurately_, so that _anyone_ reading your work will understand _exactly_ what you _mean_.

You Can Do Well _Even if You Find English Boring_

1) The _secret_ is learning the _key skills_ of studying English. Skills are like _shortcuts_ — when you know about them, they can make your life much _easier_.
2) Make sure you _read_ texts _properly_ — that means reading _carefully_ for the _important points_.
3) These skills can be used with _any_ books you read — all you need to do is _practise_.
4) _Start_ by practising with books you _like_. Remember, if you _like_ a book then you should _show_ that you like it when you _write_ about it. Look at Section Four, P.35, on comprehension skills.
5) For GCSE, you may have to read and write about books you _don't like_. If you've _practised enough_, then this _won't matter_. You'll have the _skills_ to find out the _vital information_ and to write about it in an _interesting_ way.

> REMEMBER: even if you think a book is boring, you can still write about it in an interesting way. Learn the rules for essay writing in Section Seven, P.64.

Practise _Writing Clear, Simple Personal Essays_

I'm right!   _You're wrong!_

Fred and Craig liked to give both sides of the argument

1) Personal essays always seem _much easier_ than writing about _literature_. That's why most people write very _bad_ essays, and _lose marks_.
2) You need to _learn_ the different essay _styles_ which the _Examiners_ ask for.
3) _Read_ the question _carefully_ to work out what it's _asking_ you to do.
4) If you are asked to give an _opinion_ on a topic, then give a _balanced argument_ (see P.69). Give _both_ sides of the case and then _explain why_ you would choose one side over the other.
5) If you have to write about _personal experience_, make sure you write about your _feelings_ as well as what happened. Try to make the story _come to life_ for the reader. Look at PP.82-83.

Be Prepared _for Your Coursework Deadline_

1) Your _Coursework folder_ will need to be _complete_ by a certain date.
2) That means you can write _new_ essays for it right up until the _last day_. Ask your teacher where your _problem areas_ are.
3) You _must_ include essays to fit the _categories_ given by your syllabus.
4) Ask your teacher _what_ these are — then try to _work on_ the categories where your work will receive the _lowest_ grade. You can _always_ improve your Coursework.
5) Ask your teacher if you can _rewrite_ some of your work to see if you can get _higher marks_.
6) _Don't_ leave it to the _last minute_ to improve your Coursework. If you can _keep_ working on your essays _throughout_ your course, then you'll definitely _improve_ your folder — and your _marks_.

Imagine your 'phone is cut off — you have a deadline...

There's really _no time_ to lose. If you want to do well in English or English literature, then you need to start _learning_ and _practising_ the main skills now. Each Section in this book covers a _key area_ of your course, so you must _work through_ each one. Don't forget your _Coursework_ either.

2

Standard English

Standard English is the _formal_ English that you need to use when you write in _Coursework_ or in the _Exam_. A lot of people confuse this with "speaking posh" — but it's _not_ the same thing.

Standard English is just Formal English

1) Standard English is the _form_ of English you learn in _school_.
2) All _written_ English should be standard — that means it should be _clear_ enough for _anyone_ in Britain to _understand_ it.
3) Standard English developed as the main form of _printed_ English in the _15th Century_. At the time, every _region_ of Britain used to _spell_ words _differently_, but printers needed a _fixed_ spelling.
4) Printers like _Caxton_ chose the _East Midlands_ dialect form which was used in London and the South East.
5) Soon standard English replaced all written _dialect_ forms — the _other forms_ of English spoken around the country. It also replaced _French_ and _Latin_ in _Law_ and in _academic_ work.
6) In the _18th Century_, people wrote _dictionaries_ and _grammar books_ which _standardized_ spelling — _Dr Johnson's_ _Dictionary_ of 1755 _fixed_ many of the spellings we still use today.

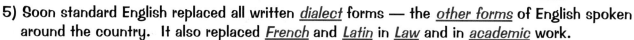
You're the most standard bloke I know Geoff

WARNING: some people say that if you don't speak standard English, then you don't speak properly. They are wrong. The important thing is being clear.

The Four Main Features of Standard English

1) All _written_ English should be _standard_ English — any _grammar_ rules you learn are for _standard_ English, and you will definitely need to _learn_ them to avoid making _mistakes_ in your work.
2) The _rules_ of standard English mean using the correct _forms_ of words with the correct _spellings_.
3) When you are doing your _Speaking_ tests, you must use the forms of _standard_ English _grammar_.
4) Your _accent_ and your _pronunciation_ don't have anything to do with standard English — the secret is avoiding any _local dialect_ words or phrases. Learn the _key grammar rules_ (P.15 on).

How to Use Standard English

How's your grammar Mr Jones?

1) Avoid _slang_ words — words that your teachers or parents wouldn't understand. You'll _lose marks_ if the _Examiners_ can't understand what you say or write.
2) Don't use _dialect_ words. Every region has _words_ or _phrases_ that are _only_ used there. _Don't_ use them in your _Coursework_, because you _won't_ be understood.
3) Make sure you revise _grammar_ and _punctuation_ in Section Three, and _learn_ the list of commonly _misspelled words_ at the end of this book.

Don't Use Clichés — You'll Lose Marks for being Boring

1) Clichés are _ideas_ or _sayings_ which have been used _so often_ that they've become _boring_ and _unoriginal_.
2) Phrases like, "As good as it gets"; "At the end of the day"; "On the other hand"; "In the fullness of time," are all _clichés_. So are images like, "as fierce as a lion"; "as cunning as a fox"; "as red as a beetroot."
3) These were all _original_ and _vivid_ images _once_, but they have been used _so often_ that they don't mean much any more.
4) If you use them, you will sound _boring_ and _unimaginative_ — that could mean you _lose marks_ for writing and speaking style. So _avoid_ clichés.

You look like you're carrying the weight of the world on your shoulders, Terry!

Standard English — sounds like a kind of fry-up...

Spend some time revising _grammar_, _spelling_ and _punctuation_ — especially if you find them tough.

Jargon and Abbreviations

Here are *two more* general points of English which people frequently *lose marks* for. Make sure you *learn* when to use them and when to *avoid* them — it could make a difference to your *grade*.

Jargon is Technical Language — Try to Avoid it

1) Jargon means language used by any *group* of people that can't be *understood* unless you're *part* of the group.
2) This means that most jargon is *meaningless* to a lot of people.
3) *Doctors*, *Lawyers*, *Teachers* and even *Poets* and *Actors* all use their own forms of jargon — special *technical* words and phrases that help them to do their jobs.
4) Different *sports* and *hobbies* also have jargon words — *football* has words like *"offside,"* or *"indirect free kick"* which don't mean anything unless you know about football.
5) *Never* use jargon in your *speaking* or *written* work — if you give a *talk*, make sure that any technical words for a hobby or a sport are *explained* so that *everyone* understands.
6) *Avoid* using *literary jargon* in essays unless you know *exactly* what the words *mean*, and can *explain* them — especially the word *"irony"* which most people use *wrongly*. There's always a *simple way* to say things — make sure your written work is always *clear* to understand.

Abbreviations are Short Forms of Words

Ned wished he had less space around him

1) Abbreviations are used to make writing *easier*. They are *shortened* forms of words which only have a *few letters*.
2) Abbreviations *don't* need *full stops* in modern usage — just leave *space* around them and *punctuate* the sentence as normal (see P.27).

Common Abbreviations You Should Learn

eg	comes from the Latin exempla gratia	=	*for example*
etc	comes from the Latin et cetera	=	*and the rest/ and so on* (*not* ect)
ie	comes from the Latin id est	=	*that is* (clarifying a point)
NB	comes from the Latin nota bene	=	*note well*
PS	comes from the Latin post scriptum	=	*for adding a note to the end of a letter*

Mr	is the short form of Mister
Ms	is used to address any woman instead of Miss or Mrs

am	comes from the Latin ante meridian	=	*before noon* (ie the morning)
pm	comes from the Latin post meridian	=	*after noon* (ie the afternoon)
BC	means Before Christ		
AD	comes from the Latin anno domini	=	*in the year of Our Lord* (eg AD 2004)

Remember the Three Rules for Abbreviations

1) *Don't* use eg, ie or etc in formal *written* work like *essays*. Only use them in *letters* or *notes*.
2) Don't confuse *eg* and *ie*; *eg* is used to give an *example* — *ie* is used to *explain* something.
3) *Never* write ect instead of etc — it's a *careless mistake* which looks sloppy.

Don't abbreviate in essays — you'll be caught short...

Three short rules for *abbreviations* to learn — and don't forget to *avoid jargon* in your work too.

What It All Means

Speaking and *Listening* are about expressing yourself clearly and showing you can *respond* to other people's ideas. That can only come with *practice*.

The Key Skills You Must Practise

1) Most people *speak too much* and *fail to communicate* important information. Their skills never improve because they don't listen properly.
2) The first key skill is learning to *listen* to people — what they're *saying* to you and also what they *don't say*. That's the only way to *respond*.
3) You need to listen to other people, to the TV or to adverts *critically* — ask yourself *why* people say certain things and *how* you should react.

4) The other key skill is *expressing yourself clearly*. That means working out the *most important* piece of information you have to communicate, and *telling* other people so that they *understand* it.
5) Talk *clearly* and *plainly* — long and fancy words are *useless* if no-one understands what you're saying.
6) Take the time to *practise* your Listening and Speaking skills — then you'll find it easier to put your ideas across clearly.
7) That will help you to sound *relaxed*, and *avoid* nervousness.
8) Practising these skills will also help your *written work* too.

How They Assess Your Skills

Most GCSE courses *assess* your Speaking and Listening skills *throughout* your course — so that means you've got to work at them *all the time*. It's very important you keep *practising*.

Getting the Best Marks

1) Oral work counts for *20%* of your final grade. You'll need to do a variety of *practical tests* in different categories but only the *best mark* in each category counts towards your final grade.
2) You must *prepare* for each practical beforehand — this will help your grade.

um....and then Columbus....um....er and then he.....er........um......

3) Spend time thinking about *how you did* afterwards — *learn* from your mistakes.
4) Make sure you know exactly *what you've got to do* for any practical — there are different *styles* of Speaking test.
5) Learn the *special skills* you need for *each style* of test — just work your way through this Section, one skill at a time.
6) Then *practise* so that you won't get nervous when you speak in front of the class.

Don't worry about the Speaking Exam — it's all talk...

Hmm... It looks like a lot to learn — and some people really hate speaking in public. Don't worry, though. If you're *organised* and you know *what to expect*, then you can face your Speaking tests with a lot of confidence. Remember — no-one wants you to do badly. The secret is being *prepared*, and *practising* as often as you can. Don't forget — it's only your *best mark* in each category that counts. That means you can have *more than one* go at each category.

Basic Speaking Skills

So here's what the Examiners are going to be testing you on in your _Speaking practicals_.

There are Three Main Categories of Practical Test

Any particular test you have to do will be assessed according to which _category_ it is in.

Categories are:

> 1) explain – describe – narrate
> 2) explore – analyse – imagine
> 3) discuss – argue – persuade

A _debate_ would be category 3. Giving a _talk_ or having a _discussion_ could fit any category, depending on the details of the activities asked for.

Teachers are asked to train students to:	A* candidates develop
1) Use standard English vocabulary and grammar	Mature and assured use of standard English
2) Listen, understand and respond appropriately to others	Perceptive listening to a range of complex speech
3) Formulate, clarify and express ideas	Understanding of challenging ideas
4) Adapt speech to a widening range of circumstances and demands	Exceptional originality and flair in adapting to task and audience

Three Talking Points to Get You Started

Think about these things _before_ you start any Speaking practical — _learn_ and remember them.

OI, YOU LOT! Shut up and listen to this!

1) **COURTESY** — Be _polite_ at all times, especially when other people ask questions, or when they're doing _their_ tests. If you're polite, they'll be on _your side_ when you do your tests.

2) **AUDIENCE** — Think about _who_ you're talking to. You'll be speaking to a big group so you have to keep people's _attention_. Tell a _joke_, or use a _visual aid_ to make your talk more interesting. _Avoid_ reading from notes — you'll _lose marks_. Just keep it short, clear and to the point.

3) **PURPOSE** — You need to get your _information across_ in an _interesting_ way, as _clearly_ as possible.

REMEMBER: CAP (Courtesy, Audience, Purpose)

Everything comes in threes — except buses...

Three categories and _three talking points_ to remember. The categories aren't very specific, which is definitely a good thing — it means you can use almost any Speaking practical in any category. Don't worry about the requirements, though. Concentrate on applying _CAP_ — think about _what_ you have to say, _who_ you're saying it to and _how_ you're going to say it.

Using Clear English

The language you use says a lot about you — and it's very important you use _clear language_ in your Speaking tests. That's why we need to talk about _standard English_ again.

Standard English is basic Formal Language

1) Everyone in Britain speaks _different versions_ of English — sometimes with _accents_ and sometimes with different _local words_ that are difficult to understand.
2) _Standard English_ is just the formal English we use that _avoids_ any local dialect words and helps people all over the country to _understand_ each other when they speak.

Speaking Clearly is Essential

1) People from different places and cultures may _pronounce_ words with different _accents_.

Oooarr, get orf my laand!

2) Accents are cool — they're part of people's _characters_ — but it's also important that everyone around the country can _communicate clearly_, whatever accent they may have.
3) Standard English developed from the form of English used for the first _printing presses_ in the late Middle Ages (for more on standard English, see P.2).
4) Remember — this _doesn't_ mean standard English is better than other dialects. The main thing is that you use it _clearly_ when you speak in _class_ and in your _Speaking practicals_.

Mad fur it aye our kid!

Use Vocab and Grammar With Care

Using standard English means following some _simple rules_.

1) _Avoid_ saying "_OK_" or "_like_" at the end of every sentence — they sound _careless_.
2) Don't use _slang_ words that some people might not understand. Slang words you use with your friends aren't always _clear_ — so think before you speak.
3) Don't use _clichés_ — corny phrases that people use all the time, without thinking. They will make you _boring_ to listen to: for example, "at the end of the day"; "sick as a parrot".
4) Watch you don't make any _grammatical mistakes_ — spend some time going over the Grammar Section of this book (see P.16 onwards):

REMEMBER — Think what you're saying: "I _was_ sitting..." NOT "I _were_ sitting..."

5) _Avoid_ using _double negatives_ in a sentence — eg "I don't never want to go back." Keep in mind that _two negatives_ make a _positive_. That means if you say "don't" _and_ "never" the negatives _cancel_ each other out, and the sentence means you _do_ want to go back.
6) When you do a Speaking Practical, _look up_ any difficult words you want to use _in advance_. Make sure you take a note of the _meaning_. If you _understand_ what a word means, you won't use it in the wrong place — and that means you _won't lose marks_.

You must speak properly — like what I does...

Time to stop and reflect — think about whether _your English_ is clear enough for the Speaking test. That _doesn't mean_ changing the way you speak, or spending years learning a posh accent. It just means checking your _grammar_, and making sure that other people can _understand_ you. Try _recording_ your own voice and listening to yourself speak — it sounds horrible but it really helps.

Holding a Conversation

Conversations are the _best way_ to practise the skills of _listening_, _understanding_ and _responding_ that will help you earn _top marks_ in your Speaking tests. So make sure you revise all this carefully.

Learn to be a Good Listener

1) _Concentrate_ on what the _other_ person is saying. This means you won't _miss_ anything and you'll make them feel more relaxed.
2) You should look them _in the eye_ and seem _interested_ in what they're saying — be an encouraging and sympathetic listener.
3) If you're unsure of a point they've made, politely _ask_ for it to be _repeated_ more clearly or _re-phrase_ it yourself, asking whether that was what the speaker meant.
4) Listen for the speaker's _tone_ — see if you can pick up their _mood_ or if their ideas sound confused. See if they repeat themselves.
5) _Don't interrupt_ speakers in mid-flow. Let them _finish_ before you have your say.

And in Response — Just be Clear and Polite

1) Respond to what the other person _actually said_ and not just what you _thought_ they said. Listen _carefully_ and _think_ before you speak.
2) Always respond _constructively_ — talk about any _good things_ that the other person said.
3) If you want to _criticise_, then be critical about their _opinion_, explaining fully _why_ you think their argument is wrong. _Never_ attack people personally — you'll _lose marks_ in a practical test.
4) If you are going to _criticise_ then you've got to be sure that _your own views_ make sense. Never criticise people if they are talking about subjects you don't understand. Ask them to _explain_.
5) _Don't be vague_ — back up anything you say with _examples_. Try to be interesting and organised in what you say. And most of all, _stick to the point_.
6) _Never generalise_ — comments like "Everyone knows" or "It's obvious" _don't help_ your case if you don't give evidence. Generalising makes people sound _arrogant_ — so don't do it.

Answering Questions — and giving Clear Answers

1) If anyone asks you a _question_ in class, make sure you _listen_ to what they ask, and try to answer it _clearly_. Be organised and _don't get flustered_.
2) Sometimes you may need to _think_ about your answer — so _ask the questioner_ if you can have some _time_ to think. Tell them you'll _come back_ to the question in a moment.
3) _Never_ allow an awkward pause — just keep going. If _you_ are speaking then you have every right to ask people with questions to _wait_ until you're finished. But do it _politely_.
4) If you use any _technical words_ then explain them as you go along, otherwise people won't understand you — for example, if you talk about rock climbing or karate.
5) Remember what you've already said — _don't contradict yourself_ (see P.68 on Argument).
6) The only way to improve is to _practise_ and to ask people for _feedback_ when it's all over.

Giving good answers — a question of practice...

Think about it — the best way to practise your speaking skills is _conversation_. Be careful, though — it's not just _talking_, but _listening_ as well. You need _both_ of these skills when you answer questions in class — always _think_ before you speak, and never _contradict_ yourself.

8

Giving A Talk

Giving a talk is a frightening business — it *isn't* always compulsory, but you still need to learn the *key skills* to help you speak in public.

Choose a Topic You Know About

1) Don't talk about topics that you *don't understand* and *can't explain* properly — choose something you *know about*.
2) This should make you more *confident* — if you know about the topic then you can be *enthusiastic* about it.
3) Then comes the really tricky part; you need to make it *interesting* for your listeners. The secret of this is *planning*.

Planning a Talk — the entertaining kind

1) *Don't* write out every single word you're going to say — your talk will just be boring. Make a *simple plan* that helps to relax you.
2) You must grab your *audience's attention* right from the start — tell a *brief story*, give a relevant *statistic* or use a *visual aid* to illustrate the *main point* of your talk. It must be really striking.
3) Once you've got their attention, you have to *keep* it. Make sure people *follow* what you say.
4) After your opening, you'll need to *introduce* your topic, *explain* what you are going to tell them and then *present* your information in a clear and logical form.
5) *Don't* look at your notes the whole time. *Watch* your audience to see if they *understand*.
6) *Explain* anything technical as you go along. Don't be afraid to *repeat* things until they are clear.
7) *Humour* is a good way to keep people's attention — but *not too much* or you can lose control of the audience. If people have *questions* then you can ask them to *wait* until you have finished.
8) Finish on a high note — *sum up* your talk and end with a story, a joke or even an appeal to people's consciences. For more details on how to prepare a *balanced argument* see P.69.

REMEMBER: *Don't* write notes in full — use *simple cards* you can read at a glance. *Avoid* reading them out — you're giving a talk to the *audience*, not to *your notes*.

You can use Props to Focus people's attention

1) There are *two kinds* of prop — the first is a *visual aid* such as a poster, video, slide show, map or diagram which you have up at the front.
2) You can use these to *illustrate* things mentioned during the talk.
3) The other kind is a *demonstration*, which can work in two ways.
4) You can perform a demonstration *at the front* — for example, making a salad or showing how to perform first aid on a classmate.
5) You can *pass* a prop *around the room* for people to look at, touch or even taste — a pet tarantula, for example, or homemade biscuits.
6) Try to choose *unusual props* but remember that *too many* will spoil the flow of the talk — and passing things around takes up a lot of time.

A good talk — more props than a rugby match...

Using props is a great way to grab people's attention — but you won't keep it unless your talk is *well planned* in the first place. Most importantly of all, *don't read* from your notes.

Giving A Talk

Phew! Now you have to do the hard part and _give_ the talk. Don't panic — you just need to know how to _present yourself_.

Presenting Yourself — Cool, Calm and Collected

Speak up!

1) _Speaking in public_ can be a big ordeal — especially if you get _nervous_. Before you give your talk, _practise_ how you'll begin. It's the hardest part.
2) Practise _speaking out loud_ by yourself — this will help you get used to _hearing_ your own voice so you won't feel so nervous. Practise any _difficult words_ in your talk so that you can pronounce them properly.
3) Best of all, _practise your talk_ in front of a few helpful friends — but make sure they're people you trust. They'll be able to tell you if you're _loud enough_ and if you kept them _interested_.
4) _Don't stress out_ if they give some critical comments — it's better that you know if there are problems with your talk _before_ the real thing, while you still have time to _change_ things around.

The Real Thing — Just keep on going

1) When you give your talk remember to _stay calm_.
2) Keep your breathing _regular_ and _even_ — if you're worried you might _dry up_, ask if you can have a _glass of water_ beside you.
3) Be _enthusiastic_ and make _eye contact_ with your audience.
4) Talk to _everybody_ in the room, not just your friends.
5) Don't be afraid to _ask_ the audience if they can all _hear_.
6) Stick to the point, and after any _long sentences_ pause to check everyone has understood.
7) If people laugh or make a noise, wait for them to _quieten down_.
8) _Stress_ any significant words and _vary_ your tone — loud or soft, fast and slow — this makes you sound more interesting.
9) _Try not_ to er and um — just take your time and speak slowly.
10) Keep your _body language_ controlled and don't fidget. Speak slowly and calmly — _don't look_ at your notes the whole time.
11) Even if something goes _wrong_, just keep on going. If you lose your place then just say so — take a deep breath and start again.
12) If you make a mistake, you _can still_ get great marks if you _react well_ and _keep talking_.

Paul found it hard to control his body language!

Taking Questions — and enjoying yourself

1) After you've _finished_ talking, there's always a time for _questions_.
2) _Be prepared_ — think about the _obvious questions_ people might ask and work out your answers _in advance_. Have the _relevant facts_ with you so that you can quote them if need be.
3) Be prepared to think _on your feet_, but _don't_ just say the first thing that comes into your head.
4) If it's a _tricky question_ ask for a moment to _think_ — then you can answer carefully (see P.7).
5) _Never make up_ an answer because you _don't know_ — be honest. No-one will expect you to know everything. Be _polite_ and _thank people_ for their attention and for their questions.

Body language — I think my stomach is growling...

Presenting yourself means _staying calm_ — which can be tough when you're giving a talk in front of the whole class. The secret is _good preparation_ — feeling comfortable with what you're going to say, and making it as _clear_ and _interesting_ as you can. That's the only way to do it.

Asking Questions

To get *top marks* in the Speaking Exam, you need to make sure that when *you do speak*, other *people listen*.

A Careful Question is Better than a Speech

Are they ready yet?

1) A good question is an effective way of *showing* that you've been *listening*, and that you have *understood* what the speaker is saying.
2) The secret is to *contribute* to the discussion or conversation in a *constructive* and *clear* way.
3) Don't ask questions to make other people look stupid. No-one likes a smart-alec — and you'll *lose marks* for distracting the class.

How to ask a Good Question

Who're you blinking tellin' to be bloomin' polite!

1) Make sure you ask a *relevant question*. If you *don't listen*, you could end up asking a really stupid question that has already been answered. Listen to *other people's* questions.
2) *Take notes* during the talk — it'll help you to *stay awake* if the talk is boring. Listen out for the *important stuff*, and make a note of anything you *don't* understand.
3) When you get the chance, ask about the things you *didn't understand*. Make sure the speaker *explains* things clearly so that the discussion can move on.
4) *Never interrupt* — wait until whoever is speaking has *finished*. If the discussion has a *chairperson*, then wait until they let you speak. Remember to be *polite*.
5) A *constructive question* is one that *develops* the discussion — a question with a yes or no answer is *not* a good one. Ask for people's *opinions*.
6) *Avoid* being *negative* — if you *disagree* with the speaker then *explain why* clearly.
7) If you are going to be *critical* then try to do it as *positively* as possible.

Don't forget: Never insult people personally, even if you think their views are wrong. It'll *lose you marks* — and people will start *criticising you*.

The Skills You're Trying to Show — Getting the Marks

1) You're really just showing that you've been *listening*.
2) You're also showing that you *understood* what was said.
3) Make sure your question is *relevant* — stick to the point.
4) Your question will show how you *reacted* to the speaker — and whether or not you're being *constructive* or just *negative*.
5) If you can show you *understood* what was said, and ask a *constructive question* that makes everybody else think and *develops* the discussion, you'll win yourself *loads of marks*.
6) As always, the secret is to *practise* — and not to talk too much.

Any questions?

Questions annoy me — they're always asking for it...

If you're going to talk in class, you may as well *pick up marks* for it. That's why you need to practise asking *constructive questions*. Then you'll make it sound like you've been *listening closely* — even when you haven't. Just remember *CAP* — what, who and how.

Having a Debate

A debate is a _formal_ discussion with firm _rules_ — make sure you know how the rules work and then you won't be caught out if you have to debate a topic.

How a Debate Works

The subject to be debated is called the _motion_ — it always takes a specific form:

> **This House believes/demands/condemns etc + whatever the topic is**

1) The Chairperson _controls_ the debate. They must be _impartial_ — they can't take sides.
2) The Chairperson _reads out_ the motion, then takes an _initial vote_ from the audience and _records_ the result. The _Proposer_ is then asked to speak.
3) During the debate the Chairperson controls _who speaks when_ and keeps the audience _quiet_ by calling for _order_. The Chairperson is the _final authority_ while the debate is going on.
4) _All speakers_ must begin their speeches with 'Mr. Chairman' or 'Madam Chairwoman'.

FOR

THE CHAIRPERSON opens the debate — ORDER! ORDER!

AGAINST

THE PROPOSER gives a speech in favour of the motion — keeping to the point and giving good reasons

THEN → **THE OPPOSER** argues against the motion — concisely and clearly, giving reasons

THE PROPOSITION SECONDER argues for the motion, supporting the proposer and arguing against the opposer

THEN → **THE OPPOSITION SECONDER** argues against the motion, supporting the opposer

Opening the Debate to the Floor

1) The Chairperson then opens the debate to the _Floor_, and anyone in the _audience_ who wants to speak can put up their hand. The Chairperson can _signal_ to them that they may speak.
2) All speakers should address the Chairperson _before_ they speak.
3) After a _few minutes_ of Floor debate, the Chairperson should ask the _Opposer_ to _sum up_ the case _against_ the motion briefly. The _Proposer_ should then _sum up_ quickly too.
4) The Chairperson takes a _final vote_ from the audience — people can vote for the motion, against it or abstain (don't know) — if a majority _supports_ the motion it is _passed_.
5) If the vote is _tied_ then the Chairperson has a _casting vote_ — deciding who wins.

Defending Your Corner

Charge!

1) _Research_ your case and work with the other person on your team.
2) _Prepare_ your speech the same way you would prepare a _talk_.
3) Use _two or three_ strong arguments with your best point for a _conclusion_.
4) You're _allowed_ to be _one-sided_ here — but use _facts_ to support your ideas.
5) Try to prove your opponents are _wrong_ — but _without_ being rude.
6) Be ready to _answer_ any criticisms they make about your arguments.

Debates are like restaurants — there are lots of orders...

Debates follow some _tricky procedures_ — make sure you know what's going to happen.

Having a Discussion

Discussions are much _less formal_ than debates — but they still have to be _constructive_.

Plan the Discussion Before You Begin

1) Usually you'll be _given a topic_ to discuss in class or in small groups. If the group has to choose its own topic then suggest something that will _interest everybody_, and about which there's _a lot to say_.
2) _Prepare_ a few ideas for _questions_ (see P.10) to start the discussion off. People may not have much to say.
3) You may need to choose a _leader_ or a _secretary_ to control who speaks when and to let everybody have their say.
4) If you are _chosen_ then you'll have to _lead_ the discussion. If not, then don't worry, you'll still have a chance to speak.

How to Lead a Discussion

Get to the point!

1) The leader's job is to _develop_ the views of the group — not to force everyone to accept their point of view.
2) Keep the discussion _to the point_. Don't let people sidetrack the group into talking about _irrelevant_ subjects.
3) _Ask questions_ — it makes people _think_ and provokes _ideas_. _Don't ask_ yes or no questions and _avoid_ asking specific individuals. It's better to ask the _whole group_.
4) Sometimes _a few members_ of the group will _dominate_ — they will want to speak all the time. Let them have their say but make sure that the _other group members_ have a _chance_ too.
5) If some people _aren't contributing_, then _invite_ them to say something — but _don't pressurise_ them. Some people just _don't want_ to take part. Your job is to give them the _opportunity_.
6) If there's an _awkward silence_ then you can _summarise_ the arguments made so far. Feel free to _contribute_ your own thoughts to the discussion, but you _mustn't_ talk all the time.

Taking Part in a Discussion — Stick to the Point

1) Be _polite_ — if you _disagree_ with someone, be _friendly_ and give your _reasons_.
2) _Agreeing_ with other people's points is a good way of moving the discussion on.
3) When you agree with someone, try to _develop_ their argument further — think about _why_ their point is valid.
4) Give _examples_ from your own _experience_, or from your _reading_, that might interest others — a story can be a _tactful_ way of presenting a _sensitive point_.
5) Remember: some people are _easily offended_ and discussions may get _emotional_ — _think_ before you speak.

6) _Listen_ to what _other people_ have to say.

Discussion time — follow the leader...

Leading a discussion is a tricky business — it looks easier than it really is. The secret is _awareness_ — keep the discussion _to the point_ and make sure everyone has a _chance to speak_.

Playing a Role

Apart from ordinary _acting_, any _discussion_ or _debate_ can also involve role-playing. The secret of all three skills is _persuading_ other people to _believe_ you.

Role Play is about _Persuading_ People to Believe You

1) _Roleplaying_ is about making people _believe you_ — especially if you're _acting_ on stage.
2) If Macbeth turns to the audience and says "Did you see the football last night?" in the middle of Shakespeare's play, we _stop believing_ that he is Macbeth straight away.

I'm the new Monstro dear boy.

Is that so sir?

3) Roleplaying is also about _arguing a point_ — in a _debate_ a speaker can _play a role_ to exaggerate an opinion. This is a great way to _involve_ an audience and can also be very _funny_ (see P.11).
4) Best of all, roleplays help you to _get inside_ other people's _characters_ — to pretend to be someone else. All literature is about getting inside _other people's heads_ and finding out what they _think about_ and what _they're like_. Roleplaying helps you develop this skill.

Using Your Imagination

1) Playing a role means using your _imagination_ to express the _emotions_ and _reactions_ of others.
2) Picture the _character_ — the setting, their clothes, personal details, emotions and attitudes — until you can imagine how they _speak_ and _behave_.
3) _Respond_ to other people _in character_ — that means _reacting_ in the way that the _character would react_: eg if you're playing a nervous person, you might faint at the slightest noise.

ROLEPLAYING could come up as part of your Speaking Exam, and it'll definitely improve your speaking skills. It'll also help you write better about drama — you can act out scenes from plays and work out how they might appear on stage.

Let your _Body_ do the _Talking_ (well, some of it)

1) Your _body language_ must fit your character.
2) Your _voice_ and your _expressions_ should reflect the _feelings_ of the character.
3) If you have a _script_, it will give _stage directions_ which tell you where to move and how to react.
4) If you're _improvising_ then _make them up_ as you go along.
5) _Respond_ to the actions of any _other characters_ in the roleplay, so that your behaviour seems _natural_.

Alas, poor Yorick...

Don't call us — we'll call you

1) Whether you're giving a _talk_, leading a _discussion_ or playing the _French Herald_ in Shakespeare's _Henry V_, you are _playing a role_ and you must _focus_ on it.
2) Ask for _feedback_ — there's always room for _improvement_, and helpful _criticism_ is essential.
3) Don't just think about your role — think about the _other characters_ in the roleplay and think about how the whole thing would _look_ and _sound_ to an audience or an assessor.

The theatre is a bakery — full of good roles...

Roleplaying isn't just about the theatre — you can use it in _all_ of your Speaking assignments. Sometimes it's easier to speak in public if you _pretend_ to be someone else — so _learn_ this page.

Revision Summary for Section Two

Your Speaking practicals don't have to be a terrible ordeal — as long as you're prepared for what you'll have to do. You're trying to persuade people — to listen to you and to believe you. Look at P.81 on Rhetoric to give you some ideas on how to use language to persuade you. You should also look back at P.2 on standard English — don't forget to avoid using any dialect words or slang when you speak in class. People only become good at public speaking through practice, and that takes time. Just learn to prepare properly and practise speaking out loud on your own. Look at these questions to remind yourself of the key points in this Section — make sure you've learned them all carefully.

1) What three things do you have to think about before you start any Speaking practical?
2) What is standard English? Are dialect words part of standard English?
3) Is your accent important when you speak?
4) Why do you need to use standard English when you speak in class?
5) Why should you avoid double negatives when you speak?
6) In conversations and discussions, what should you do if you don't understand what someone has said?
7) What should you do if you don't agree with what someone has said? What should you never do when you criticise someone else's remarks?
8) What is the secret to giving an interesting and successful talk?
9) Should your notes give every word of your talk?
10) Should you look at your notes while you give your talk?
11) Give five things you can do to present yourself well when you speak.
12) How would you prepare for taking questions after your talk?
13) What should your questions do in a discussion?
14) What are the six secrets of asking good questions?
15) What does the chairperson do in a debate?
16) What does the Proposer do?
17) What does the Opposer do?
18) What do the seconders do? When do they speak?
19) How should you address the chairperson in a debate?
20) When can people in the audience start contributing to a debate?
21) What should the leader of a discussion do if people aren't joining in?
22) What should they do if there's an awkward silence?
23) How would you prepare for a role play?
24) Why is it important to stay in character?
25) How can you practise your public speaking skills? Why should you practise?

Making Grammar Easy

Let's face it, grammar is boring. The trouble is, you can _lose loads of marks_ if you _can't spell_ and if you make _silly grammatical mistakes_.

This Section is about Picking up the Easy Marks

1) We _already know_ most of the rules of grammar _instinctively_ — we use them whenever we speak or write, but perhaps no-one has ever _explained_ them in grammatical terms.

2) _Grammar_ is just the _group of rules_ that help us to use words correctly in a language. _Syntax_ is about putting words together in _sentences_.

3) You only need to know the _key rules_ of grammar and punctuation to help you avoid _mistakes_ that could _lose you marks_ in your work.

4) It'll help you write more _precisely_, more _clearly_ and more _accurately_ — and that will win you extra marks. You will also start to recognise the ways in which _authors_ use language for effect.

The secret of grammar is making sure you know how different words work — what their function is in a sentence and how you choose the right form to use.

The Verb is used to describe an Action

1) The _verb_ tells us _what_ is happening and _when_. It is the _'DOING'_ word of a sentence.

2) Verbs _change_ their _form_ and are sometimes formed using the auxiliary verbs 'to have', 'to be', 'will' and 'shall', according to _when_ the action is taking place. These changed verb forms are called _tenses_.

eg	I _go_ to town	The action is happening _now_	= _present_ tense
	I _went_ to town	The action has _already_ happened	= _past_ tense
	I _shall go_ to town	The action _hasn't_ happened _yet_	= _future_ tense

Read through and then scribble your own _copy_ of this _table of tenses_ using a different verb:

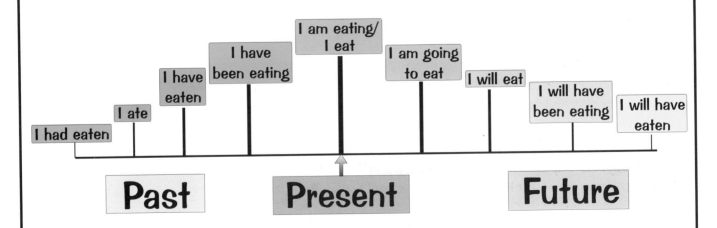

Grammar is about rules — so's Granpa...

There are _thirty rules_ in this Section on _grammar_, _spelling_ and _punctuation_. That sounds like a lot, but if you can learn _one_ every day, that'll take _thirty days_ — which is a month. So in _one month_ you can definitely _improve_ your written work — that means _fewer mistakes_ and _more marks_.

To Be (or not To Be)

The verb _to be_ is the most important verb in English and it's really very easy to use, as long as you avoid making a few _obvious mistakes_.

Learn the _Simple Present_ and _Past_ forms of 'to be'

You use this verb all the time, so if you're _writing_ these forms wrongly you must be _saying_ them wrongly. Make sure you know the basic forms.

Present:

> I am
> You are
> He/She/It is
> We are
> You are
> They are

Past:

> I was
> You were
> He/She/It was
> We were
> You were
> They were

→

> I, You, He/She/It
> = singular
>
> We, You, They
> = plural

NB: The word '_you_' has a singular and a plural form — it can mean one person or a whole group.

When to use _Were_ and when to use _Was_

People often say '_I were_' instead of '_I was_', or '_we was_' instead of '_we were_'. These forms are not correct in formal English. Anyone who uses them in an _essay_ or an _Exam_ will automatically _lose marks_. The rule is simple:

> **_RULE 1:_** you must use were with all plural forms and always with you — singular and plural. Only I, he, she and it take was.

There is one _exception_ to this rule. In phrases with '_if_', you can use _were_ with _I_, _he_, _she_ or _it_.
> eg   If I _were_ you...   If only she _were_ a better singer...
Remember this is only in the one special case.

> Don't confuse were with we're — were is part of the verb to be, but we're is the short form of we are (see page 28).

A Terrible Mistake — 'Been' and 'Being'

These are two words that _sound_ very similar and can easily be _confused_. Fortunately there's a very practical way of _telling them apart_:

> **_RULE 2:_** you can only use been with have, has or had in front of it. Being must have another part of the verb to be — is, am, are, was, or were.

> eg   I had _been_ to the shops — the action happened in the _past_ and was _completed_.
> I have _been_ unwell — the action was in the _recent past_ and may still be going on.
> I am _being_ followed — the action _is happening_ right now.
> I was _being_ chased — the action _was still going on_ at the moment described.

The boring technical explanation for this rule is that _being_ is the _present participle_, _been_ is the _past participle_ — but you don't need to learn that. Just learn the rule and _don't confuse_ the two forms.

> Don't forget — '_been_' and '_being_' are used to help form some tenses of other verbs:
> eg   I have _been_ eating dog food.
> Heathcliff had _been_ gone for years.
> He is _being_ watched.

> Stop being daft!

> I always have been.

Mistakes with the Verb 'Have'

The verb *'to be'* and the verb *'to have'* are auxiliary verbs — this means they <u>combine</u> with other verbs to form <u>different tenses</u> (eg I was shopping, he has crashed).

A Multi-talented Verb — 'to have'

1) The verb *'to have'* is used to mean <u>possessing</u> something, as well as to form several <u>tenses</u>.

2) The <u>present</u> tense of 'to have' (have, has) is added to a verb to form a <u>past</u> tense where the action was quite <u>recent</u> — I <u>have bought</u> a new jacket (see verb table on P.15).

3) The <u>past</u> tense of 'to have' (had) is added to a verb to form the <u>pluperfect</u> — I <u>had</u> eaten.

You must say 'I did' or 'I have done' — never 'I done'

1) There are two confusing ways to talk about actions you completed in the <u>past</u>:

I did learn not to say I done

> ### You can use '<u>I did</u>' or '<u>I have done</u>'

'I did' emphasises that the action was a <u>single</u> past event.
'I have done' suggests that the action was more <u>recent</u> in the past.

2) Don't confuse the two — you'll lose lots of <u>valuable marks</u>:

> ### Some people say 'I done' — this is wrong

3) Remember — *'done'* isn't a verb form on its own: it's only <u>part</u> of a verb. Learn the forms.

I did		I have done
You did		You have done
He/She/It did	***Or***	He/She/It has done
We did		We have done
You (plural) did		You (plural) have done
We did		They have done

Remember that <u>He</u>, <u>She</u> and <u>It</u> use <u>has</u> instead of <u>have</u>.

4) To avoid this mistake, make sure you learn the <u>simple rule</u>:

> **<u>RULE 3:</u>** 'has', 'have' or 'had' must <u>always</u> go before 'done' in the past tenses. There are **NO EXCEPTIONS** to this rule, so learn it and don't forget it.

eg   She <u>did</u> the only thing she could.   Katy <u>has done</u> her best.

The Short Form of <u>Could Have</u> <u>is</u> Could've

1) The words <u>could</u>, <u>should</u>, <u>would</u>, and <u>might</u> are used with the verb form *'have + verb'*, to say that something might have been possible in the past — each has a different shade of meaning:

eg I could <u>have escaped</u> to Florida if the RAF hadn't forced me to land the 747.

Parts of Verb

2) Many people say *'could of'* instead of *'could have'*. This is totally <u>wrong</u>. The *'have'* is part of the verb form that follows (eg have escaped) — it <u>doesn't</u> go with the verb *'could'*.

3) The correct short form for <u>could have</u> is *'could've'* — but you should <u>never</u> use it in formal <u>written</u> English, only for writing <u>dialogue</u>. It sounds like could of but it <u>isn't</u> — remember:

> **<u>RULE 4:</u>** could've is short for could have because have is part of the verb that follows — the same goes for might've, would've and should've.

4) The word *'of'* is not part of a verb, so never use it that way — see P.23.

5) For the <u>differences</u> between could, should, would, might etc, see next page.

Being able to; Shall/Will; Should/Would

Can, may, might, shall, will, could, would and should are _confusing_ so study this page carefully.

Can means 'being capable of doing'

1) The word can is used in the _present_ tense to mean being _able_ to do something — the action is something which will be _possible:_ eg When I leave school I _can_ travel.

2) It also means a _physical ability:_
   eg I _can_ touch my toes. In Mexico the beans _can_ jump.

3) The _opposite_ of can is _cannot_, which has the short form _can't_. In your essays you must only use _'cannot'._

4) In the _past_ tense, can becomes _could_ — although could is also used as a polite form in asking other people questions:
   eg _Could_ you pass me the salt please?

5) The phrase _'could + have done'_ is used to talk about an action that _was possible_ in the past (see P.17).

6) The _opposite_ of could is _could not,_ or _couldn't:_
   eg He _couldn't_ finish his lunch yesterday.

That bean sure can jump!

May is used for Possibility and Permission

1) The word _may_ is used for _asking permission:_ eg _May_ I leave the room, please?

2) Lots of people use _'can'_ here but it is _wrong_ — 'Can I leave the room?' means 'Am I capable of leaving the room?' _Don't_ make this mistake.

3) _May_ is also used to say something is _possible_ — but only if it is _likely_ to happen:
   eg I _may_ be going to see United at the weekend.

Might is used for Possibilities that are Less Likely

Might is used with _possibilities_, but only when something is _unlikely_ to happen:
   eg Next year I _might_ be discovered and asked to star in an Hollywood film with Arnie.

Shall and Will are "Used" to Form the Future Tense

1) Shall and will are _auxiliary_ verbs. Shall is used with _'I'_ and _'we'_; will is used with _you, he, she, it_ and _they:_
   eg I _shall_ go sailing. You _will_ be leaving soon.

2) If you want to _stress_ a point, you can use _will_ with _'I'_ and _'we'_, and _shall_ with _you, she, he, it_ and _they:_
   eg I _will_ go sailing. You _shall_ go to the ball.

3) Many people don't use these forms this way — you probably won't lose marks if you don't. _Will_ is also used as a _noun._

You shall go to the ball!

Should and Would are Past Tense Forms

1) _Should_ is the past tense form of _'shall'_, and is used to show when something is a _necessary task_ (a duty) or when something is very _likely:_ eg You _should_ apologise. They _should_ be home soon.

2) _Would_ is the _past_ tense and _conditional_ tense of the verb _'will'_. It is used in the _past_ tense to talk about something in the _future:_ eg He said he _would_ go. = past of 'he says he _will_ go.'
   It is also used to show _willingness:_ eg I _would_ like to come. _Would_ you like a drink?
   It can also show a _habit:_ eg He always _would_ complain about the weather.

3) _Don't_ confuse would and should — remember the _rule:_

RULE 5: only use should when it's necessary or likely; would has lots of uses.

Nouns and Pronouns

We only need to go over nouns and pronouns quickly, so that you can avoid the _big mistakes_.

Nouns are for Naming People and Things

1) Any word that names an _animal_, _person_, _place_ or _thing_ in a sentence is a _noun_.

2) _Nouns_ can be used in _two ways_:

> The SUBJECT of a sentence is the person or thing that does or is something
> The OBJECT of a sentence is the person or thing that has something done to it

eg   The _Sheriff_ arrested _Juan_

      SUBJECT   OBJECT

It's not me!
It's the
other Juan.

3) The names of _people_, _organisations_ or particular _places_ are called _proper nouns_ — remember to write them with a _capital letter_: eg   Miles Davis, Newcastle United, Scotland.

Pronouns Replace Nouns to Avoid Repetition

1) Pronouns are words like _he_, _she_ or _it_, used to avoid repeating the noun over and over.   This is because it sounds clumsy to _repeat_ the noun, especially a long word or a proper name.
eg   _Juan_ robbed the bank. _Juan_ hid the money in the desert. The sheriff came to look for _Juan_.

2) In the second sentence, the noun Juan is the _subject_ so it can be replaced by the pronoun _he_.

3) In the third sentence, the noun Juan is the _object_ so it can be replaced by the pronoun _him_.

Here is a list of some basic pronoun forms — don't get them confused:

SUBJECT	OBJECT	SUBJECT	OBJECT	SUBJECT	OBJECT
I	— me	she	— her	we	— us
you	— you	he	— him	they	— them
		it	— it		

> _RULE 6:_ when the noun is a subject, use a subject pronoun; when it's an object, use an object pronoun. When nouns stand for things, they take it or they.

eg   _They_ smiled at _us_ more than _we_ smiled at _them_.   _She_ likes _him_ and _he_ likes _her_.

When to use You and I and when to use You and Me

1) This is one people always get muddled up — but it's very _easy_ if you know your _pronoun table_.

> Use 'you and I' when both words are the subject of the sentence.
>> eg   _You and I_ need to have a word.
>
> Use 'you and me' when both words are the object of the sentence.
>> eg   Dave came to look for _you and me_.

2) Many people say 'Dave came to look for you and I', which is _incorrect_. Learn the rule:

> _RULE 7:_ when you have a choice between you and I and you and me, write the sentence out twice — once using only the word I and once using only the word me. Only one form will make sense — I must _always_ be a subject.

3) After all _prepositions_ (see P.22) you must always use '_me_':   eg _between_ you and _me_.

4) This is true for _all_ pronouns that have _different_ subject and object forms (her, us, them etc):
eg   _The lead singer and he are very alike._   _Sandy came after you and her in the queue._

Describing and Comparing

Adjectives and *adverbs* are just *descriptive* words — adjectives describe nouns, while adverbs describe verbs and adjectives. The problem here comes when you try to *compare* things.

Use Adjectives to Describe Nouns

1) Adjectives *describe* nouns or pronouns. They give you more information about the noun, and help to make a piece of writing clearer and more vivid.
   eg 'There was a big, grey horse', is a much clearer image than just saying 'There was a horse'.

2) Most adjectives come *before* the noun they describe.

3) When an adjective is used with the verb 'to be', it can be *separated* from the noun.

4) In certain set phrases, adjectives *follow* the noun instead.

Anne has a *broken* ankle.
The *vicious* dragon attacked them.
This ship is too *small*.
That officer has been *brutal*.
court *martial*,
mission *impossible*, etc.

Adverbs Describe Verbs and Adjectives

1) Adverbs describe *how* an action was performed:
   eg She danced *energetically*. He ate *quickly*.
2) They also describe *adjectives* — eg *happily* married.
3) Most adverbs *end* in the letters *-ly*. Be careful though; some *adjectives* also end in -ly:
   eg lovely, lively, friendly.
4) Look at the example on the right:

So I said to Noel Coward "Those are the wrong trousers"

How witty!

A *truly witty* man can tell an *expertly timed* joke, without being *really rude* to anyone.

Comparisons — using more and most or -er and -est

1) When you want to *compare things*, use *more* + adjective/adverb + *than*.
   eg He is *more charming than* his friend. She danced *more energetically* with Paul *than* with you.

   OR you can add *-er* + *than* to the end of *short*, everyday words.
   eg Robert is a lot *taller* than Andrew. This question is *harder* than the last one.

2) There isn't a precise *rule* for when you should use -er, but generally you should use it with short words that have only *one syllable*. Watch out for irregular forms — see next page.

3) The word *than* is used to introduce the *second* thing you are comparing. Sometimes it is left out — this is because it is taken as understood already. *Don't* do this in your written work.
   eg My debt is now a lot *smaller*. She seems *happier*.

4) Make sure you learn the *rule* for comparatives:

RULE 8: Never use more and -er together when you compare things. Use -er with shorter words and some special cases. Otherwise use more + adjective/adverb. Always use than to introduce the second thing you are comparing.

5) When you want to say something is the *best*, or highest quality, use *most* in front of the adjective, or *-est* at the end of the *short* adjective — these are called *superlative forms*:
   eg It is the *richest* country in the World. Of all the volunteers, he is the *most willing* to help.

6) The superlative form does not use *'than'*. It is only used to compare *three* or *more* things.

How to Use Descriptive Words

Time to make sure that you're clear on those _comparatives_ and _superlatives_ — learn the table.

Table of Comparatives and Superlatives

	Comparative adj./adv.	Superlative adj./adv.	
good (adjective) well (adverb)	better	best	
bad (adjective) badly (adverb)	worse	worst	
much (adj./adv.)	more	most	* Fewer and fewest also exist. The adverbial
few* (adjective)	less	least	equivalent of few is little.

The Two Key Rules for Using Adjectives and Adverbs

Using adjectives and adverbs will help you develop a _good written style_ — they make your work more _interesting_ and _precise_ for the Examiner. There are two important rules for using them:

> **1) When you use words like _beautiful_, _lovely_ and _wonderful_, you must explain _why_ you have used them. Without explanation they are meaningless.**

It's not specific enough to say 'This poem is beautiful'. You must _explain why_ it is beautiful:

> eg   "Anyone lived in a pretty how town" by E.E. Cummings, is a poem about time passing in a small town. It is beautiful because the rhythm of the words is like a chiming church bell.

Avoid words that you _can't explain_ — the Examiner will just think that you are _confused_.

> **2) Avoid _technical-sounding_ words like _realistic_, _important_, _poetic_ or _stylish_, unless you can explain _why_ you're using them. This is a very common mistake.**

People often write things like, '_Wuthering Heights_ is a very poetic novel'. This means _nothing_ unless you can explain _why_ it is poetic:

> eg   ...because it creates images of the passions of love and despair in the face of the great power of nature, in a similar way to many Romantic poems from the early 19th century.

If you can use your _adjectives_ and _adverbs_ to link into specific _examples_, you will start to write _clear_, _stylish_ essays — which means the Examiner will enjoy them and give you _more marks_.

Improving Your Style — Vocab and Practice

1) Writing well means using words _accurately_ and being _clear_.
2) Improving your written work should include learning _new_ words — as many as you can. You must learn the _meaning_ and the _spelling_ of any new words carefully.
3) Whenever you're _reading_ and you find a word you don't know, _write it down_ and _look it up_ in a dictionary. Practise spelling it and start trying to use it — but make sure you use it _correctly_.
4) _Don't_ use words if you're not sure what they _mean_; you will _lose marks_ if you use words inaccurately in your work.
5) If you're in doubt about a word, find the _clearest_ way of saying _what you mean_. There's an _easy_ way to say everything.
6) If you use a _difficult_ or a _technical_ word, you should explain what it means in _brackets_ (see P.30 on the use of brackets).

RTA on the A595, ETA 15. Get them into crash ASAP.

?!

Joining Words and Relationship Words

There are two more types of word you need to know about — they are both forms of _linking_ word, and their job is to _connect_ the different parts of a sentence.

Conjunctions are the basic joining words

1) These are words like _and_ or _but_ which join words or phrases in a sentence. They are used to form _longer_ sentences:

    eg   The army tried to advance, _but_ after a few yards the horses and cannon became stuck in the mud.

2) Common conjunctions are:

    and, but, although, as soon as, because, either, or, that, though, which, who, etc.

3) Be very _careful_ when you use conjunctions, especially at the _start_ of a sentence.

Never begin a sentence with the words _and_ or _but_

This is something that will _lose_ you _easy marks_ in your Exam work — so avoid this mistake.

> 1) _Never_ begin a sentence with _and_ or _but_ — just don't do it.

This is _easy_ if you think about it: a conjunction joins two words or phrases, but there's _nothing_ to join a word with at the _beginning_ of a sentence — so you _can't possibly_ use and or but.

> 2) Sometimes you may read sentences beginning with _because_ or _although_ with a main clause following them — these sentences are used for _emphasis_, but _don't_ do it in _your_ written work. You will _lose marks_ if you do.

a) Here the order of the _main_ clause and the _dependent_ clause have been _changed_ for emphasis:

    Although he is good, he doesn't train hard enough.   _Because_ I am a Martian, I am green.

    is an _emphatic_ version of ⬇   is an _emphatic_ version of ⬇

He doesn't train hard enough although he is good.   I am green because I am a Martian.

MAIN CLAUSE   DEPENDENT CLAUSE   MAIN CLAUSE   DEPENDENT CLAUSE

b) It's called the _dependent_ clause because it _depends_ on the _main_ clause.

> **RULE 9:** never use but, and or because to begin a sentence in written work.

Prepositions — Words that show Relationships

1) Prepositions are words that show the _relation_ of a noun or pronoun to another word. This means that they show _where_ things are in relation to each other:

    eg   _on, at, near, with, onto, to, of._

2) Most prepositions have different _meanings_ in different _situations_ — but don't worry, you only need to know how to avoid the most _common mistakes_ with prepositions (see next page).

3) _Don't forget_ — if a preposition is followed by a _pronoun_, it will always be an _object_ pronoun (see P.19).

I was caught on camera at the bank with the money

Mistakes with 'of', 'from' and 'to'

Three very annoying little _mistakes_ to avoid here — make sure you _learn_ how to spot the _traps_.

Two _tricky_ little words — _don't confuse of/off_

1) _Off_ gives the idea of being _away_ from something — going away, coming away or being taken away from something,   eg a price can have twenty percent _off_.
2) It's also used in some _specific phrases_: eg Come _off_ it! The plane took _off_. The milk was _off_.
3) _Of_ is a _linking_ word in a sentence — a _preposition_ — meaning various things, including possession, origin, cause and about:
    eg A friend _of_ mine.   The works _of_ Shakespeare.   He died _of_ shame.   Let's talk _of_ other things.

REMEMBER: off is about being away and has two 'ff's — of is a preposition. Think what you are trying to say before you use either one in a sentence.

You must use 'different from' — _don't use 'different to'_

1) Another really irritating error which _loses you marks_ — many people use '_different than_' or '_different to_' in their written work. This is _incorrect_. The only correct form is '_different from_'.
2) This makes sense if you learn the rule:

    Different means '_not the same_' — meaning _separate_ from the thing described.

    eg   Jane is very _different from_ Rochester.   Holden thinks he is _different from_ other teenagers.

3) '_Different to_' is wrong because '_to_' means '_going towards_' — which is the complete opposite of the idea of '_separation from_'. 'Different' and 'to' _contradict_ each other.
4) '_Different than_' is an _American_ form, and that means it is _wrong_ to use it in your written work.

Two/to/too — _they Don't Mean the Same thing_

1) These three words are easily _confused_ because they all _sound the same_ — be very careful.
2) _Two_ is a _number_ — just think of the word _twice_: eg   There were _two_ ravens.
3) _Too_ means _also_ — remember that you need to add an '_o_' for also: eg   I ate _too_ much.
4) _To_ is a _preposition_ meaning _towards_, or part of a _verb_: eg   I went _to_ town. You went _to_ eat.

RULE 10: to means to-wards or is part of a verb; too adds an 'o' to mean 'also'; two is a number — so think twice.

'To Try To' — _a Phrase to Remember_

1) The verb '_to try_' is used with the _infinitive form_ of other verbs: eg to do, to eat, to see.
2) It is _never_ used in the phrase '_to try and_'. This is completely _wrong_ and will _lose marks_.
3) You must _always_ use the form '_to try to_':   eg   She decided _to try to_ become a star.

A Short Note on Separation

Separation is a word that people often _spell incorrectly_ — eg seperation. In fact it's very _easy_ to ensure you get it right _every_ time, if you learn the rule:

RULE 11: Separation means apart, so spell it with par.

Avoiding Common Spelling Mistakes

You'll really _lose marks_ for _bad spelling_ in the Exam — so _learn_ these simple rules.

The Top Two Spelling Rules for the letter 'e'

1) Use _'i'_ before _'e'_ except after _'c'_ — but just when it rhymes with _'bee'_.

When you try to spell a word with an _'e'_, say it in your head and think about whether the _'ie'_ part sounds like _'bee'_. This is the easy way to make _sure_ you _spell_ these words _correctly_.

eg

believe	➡	the 'ie' sounds like bee
thief	➡	the 'ie' sounds like bee
achieve	➡	the 'ie' sounds like bee

but:

leisure	➡	'ei' doesn't sound like bee
weight	➡	'ei' doesn't sound like bee
receive	➡	use 'ei' because of the 'c'

There are a few key _exceptions_ to this rule:

Weird, _weir_ and _seize_ sound like bee _but_ use 'ei'.

Science has an 'ie' that _does_ follow a 'c'.

People's _names don't_ follow the rules: eg Keith.

i before e and look there's a c....ha ha ha!!!

> _IMPORTANT NOTE:_ remember to learn the correct spellings for 'neither' and 'either', because they can be pronounced in two different ways (to rhyme with bee or to rhyme with eye).

Another useful rule for the letter 'e' is when it comes at the end of a word:

2) Chop off the 'e' at the end of a word when you add _-ing_, except when there's a double '-e' where you just add -ing.

eg   dance ➡ dancing   wake ➡ waking   _but_   flee ➡ fleeing   see ➡ seeing

Changing the forms of words ending in '-y'

1) Lots of words end in 'y', whether _nouns_ like 'day', _verbs_ like 'hurry' or _adjectives_ like 'happy'.

2) There are _two rules_ for changing the forms of these words:

> _RULE 12:_ If the letter before the -y is a vowel — a, e, i, o, u — the -y remains.
> eg buy ➡ buyer   key ➡ keys   day ➡ days   obey ➡ obeys
>
> _RULE 13:_ If the letter before the -y is a consonant, the -y is replaced by an -i.
> eg hurry ➡ hurries   easy ➡ easier   daisy ➡ daisies   happy ➡ happiest

Don't forget — these examples are all sorts of _different_ word forms. The word _'daisy'_ is a _noun_; _'happy'_ is an _adjective_; _'hurries'_ is a _verb_. The _only_ thing you need to learn here is the _spelling rule_ — when to _change_ the -y at the end of a word to an -i, and when to _leave_ it alone.

Let's take a break — it's time for a recap...

Lots of _rules_ to remember here — time to go over a few of the key points. Start by looking at _verb forms_, especially when they involve the _auxiliary verbs_ 'to be' and 'to have'. You must always remember to use _'could have'_, never 'could of'.

The tricky part about _nouns_ and _pronouns_ is knowing the _difference_ between _subjects_ and _objects_. Look through p.19 again if you're not sure. Think carefully about what you mean to say when you're using _adjectives_ — don't forget your _comparatives_. _Prepositions_ are pretty easy to use, the problems come when you get simple swords muddled up.

Phew! I know it looks like a lot, but you'll be fine if you know the _key rules_. Go over the first half of this Section now, and write down all the rules. Then spend some time learning them.

SECTION THREE — GRAMMAR AND PUNCTUATION

More Spelling Tips

A _varied_ vocabulary will definitely improve your Essay-writing, but if you spell words _wrongly_ over and over, then you can guarantee that the Examiner will take marks _away_ from your work.

Watch out for these Four Silly Spelling Mistakes

1) Words that have a 'y' in the middle, especially 'rhythm' and 'rhyme'.
2) Words with a silent 'h' — you don't say it, but you must write it: eg chemistry.
3) Words written with 'ph' and pronounced with an 'f':   eg graph or philosophy.
4) Never end any word with '-ley' except if it is a place name: eg Headingley.

Words that Sound the Same but have Several Spellings

The words below are _regularly confused_ in written work. Make sure that you know how to use them _correctly_.

I love spelling!

1) affect/effect

1) _Affect_ is a _verb_ meaning to act on or _influence_ something
2) _Effect_ is a _noun_ — it is the _result_ of an action
3) _Effect_ can also be used as a _verb_ meaning to _achieve_

eg

Global warming is _affecting_ Earth's climate.   The _effect_ of global warming is climate change.

= influencing/acting on   = result   = influence/act on

= achieved

He _effected_ his escape through a secret tunnel.   His escape didn't _affect_ me.

There are other meanings of affect but they are not important at this stage.

2) practise/practice

1) _Practise_ is a _verb_ meaning to make a _habit_ of, to _work_ at something or to work in a profession:
   eg   He tries to _practise_ what he preaches. I _practise_ the piano daily. She _practises_ medicine.
2) _Practice_ is a _noun_ meaning the _effort_ of improving a skill, the usual _way_ something is done, an _action_ or _performance_ or the _business_ of a professional:
   eg   I enjoy football _practice_.   The _practice_ of polygamy is rare nowadays.
         Practice makes perfect.   Dr. Killer only has a small medical _practice_ now.

3) where/were/wear

1) _Where_ is used to talk about _place_ and _position_: eg   _Where_ is the Frenchman?
2) _Were_ is a _past tense_ form of the verb '_to be_' (see P.16):   eg They _were_ hidden behind a statue.
3) _Wear_ is a _verb_ used with clothes, hair, jewellery etc: eg He _wears_ armour of burnished gold.

4) there/their/they're

1) _There_ is used for _place_ and _position_ — remember _where_ and _there_ go together.
2) _Their_ shows _possession_ — that something _belongs_ to them.
3) _They're_ is the short form for '_they are_' — see the section on _apostrophes_ (see P.28).
   eg   I went there to meet their friends. They're very charming people.

5) stationary/stationery

1) _Stationary_ with an '_a_' means motionless or _still_.   Remember; stationary means cars and vans.
2) _Stationery_ with an '_e_' means _office equipment_.   Learn this; stationery means pens and pencils.

A Mark-Saving Page

Here are some common words that people often get _mixed up_ — so learn the simple rules.

Don't use Them when you mean Those

1) Sometimes people try to use the word _'them'_ as an _adjective_: eg   Let me see _them_ books.
2) This is _wrong_; them is the _object pronoun_ from the word _they_ (see P.19):   eg   I met _them_.
3) The word _those_ must be used instead: eg   Let me see _those_ books.

> **RULE 14:** never use them together with a noun — you must always use those.

Who is for People and Which is for Animals and Things

Who and _which_ are _pronouns_ used to _join_ two phrases together — they are very _easy_ to use.

> **RULE 15:** who is used to talk about people; which is used for animals or things.

   eg   King Lear had two daughters _who_ lied to him.   Androcles met a lion _which_ did not kill him.

Remember — the pronoun who changes to _whom_ with _prepositions_:

   eg   He was a general for _whom_ soldiers would do anything.   To _whom_ am I speaking?

As and Like follow a Strict, Simple Rule

> **RULE 16:** like is always followed by a noun or a pronoun on its own; as is followed by a noun with a verb.

   eg   Othello did _as_ Iago told him.   She looks _like_ him.   He sings _like_ an angel.

1) _Don't forget_ — you _can't_ use like in place of as: Othello did _like_ Iago told him = _WRONG_.
2) Some people say _'like'_ at the _end_ of a sentence: eg   He seemed a bit confused, like.
3) This sounds odd in _formal_ English and you should _never_ write it — you'll definitely _lose marks_.

When to use Lend and when to use Borrow

1) These words are easily _confused_, but in fact they are _opposites_ in meaning.
2) _Lend_ means to _give_ something out for a while; _borrow_ means to _take_ something for a time.
3) Learn the simple _rule_:

> **RULE 17:** you lend something to a person or borrow it from them.

   eg   John has _lent_ me his new Ferrari.   She has _borrowed_ my shotgun for her wedding.

The difference between Teach and Learn

> **RULE 18:** the verb to teach means giving out knowledge; learning means taking knowledge in. Don't muddle the two.

Between is always followed by 'and'

1) People often try to write 'between him _or_ her'. This is _incorrect_.
2) Make sure you _always_ use _'and'_ with between:
   eg She must choose between Leo _and_ Matt.
3) _Remember_ that _between_ always takes _object_ pronouns (see P.19 and P.22):
   eg   between _you_ and _me_,   between _you_ and _her_.

Darling,
Between you and me, your dinner is in the dog.
Love
Sweety Pie.
xxx

Yum, yum!!

Punctuation

Punctuation is the collection of _symbols_ used to _break up_ groups of words. They make words easier to read and to understand — so you need to know how to _recognise_ them and _use_ them in your own writing.

Closing a Sentence — the Full Stop

1) Full stops mark a definite _pause_ at the _end_ of a sentence.
2) A _sentence_ is a group of words that makes sense on its own
   — it usually contains a _subject_ and a _verb_.
3) A sentence asking a _direct question_ is closed with a _question mark_: eg Where are you going?
4) If the sentence tells you _about_ a question but _doesn't_ ask it, then it is an _indirect question_ and has a _full stop_: eg The reader asked the rider where he was going.
5) _Exclamation marks_ are used to _emphasise_ sentences — to show a strong _reaction_ or to give an _order_: eg I don't believe it! Hold your fire!

> **RULE 19:** don't use too many exclamation marks — they are only for special cases of emphasis. Never use more than one at a time.

A Comma is a pause in the middle of a sentence

1) Commas are used to _separate_ words or groups of words so that the _meaning_ is made _clear_:
   eg   In the valley below, the villages seemed very small.
   Without a comma, the sentence would say, 'the valley below the villages' — a _different_ meaning.
2) In very _long_ sentences they come _before_ the joining word '_and_' or '_but_'.

Clean pause...

3) They are also used to _separate_ items in a _list_ — the _last two_ items _don't_ have a comma but must be joined by the words '_and_' or '_or_':
   eg I went to buy onions, mushrooms, peppers _and_ pasta.
4) They can be used to separate _additional_ phrases or words added to a sentence to give _extra information_ or effect, but which aren't _essential_:
   eg The murderer, therefore, must be Miss Marble.
       I fell in love with Juliet, who is alas a Capulet, at the party last night.

Using Semi-Colons and Colons

Semi-Colons link related sentences

You're not half the colon I am!

1) Semi-colons are _halfway_ between _full-stops_ and _commas_.
2) They _link_ two sentences with a _similar meaning_ and turn them into _one longer_ sentence. The two parts either side of the semi-colon should be _equally important_.
   eg   She was trying to defuse the bomb but the control box contained three wires; she couldn't decide whether to cut the red one, the green one or the blue one.
3) Semi-colons can _also_ be used in writing _lists_ — here the last two items _don't_ need an _and_ or _or_.
   eg   The price includes: starter; fish course; sorbet; main course; dessert; cheese; coffee.

> **RULE 20:** use a semi-colon when the two parts of a sentence are equally important; if the first part leads on to the second part you must use a colon.

Colons divide sentences and introduce lists

1) Colons are used to _divide_ sentences in two when the second half _explains_ the first half:
   eg   The ballroom had become very empty: most of the guests had left.
2) It allows the writer to _illustrate_ or _explain_ a point — to say the same thing and make it _clearer_.
3) Colons can also be used to _introduce_ a list, but each part of the list must _make sense_ by itself.

Apostrophes

Apostrophes always seem to cause massive problems — so *learn these rules* to stay out of trouble.

Apostrophes can show *Possession*

1) Apostrophes are used to show *possession* — when a person *owns* something:
   eg The Queen's English is posh. Orwell's vision of the future was wrong about the right things.

> **RULE 21:** an apostrophe of possession must come before or after at least one s.

2) To *use* an apostrophe you must decide what the *basic* word is *without* one. In the examples above, the basic words are the *Queen* and *Orwell*. Then add apostrophe and 's':

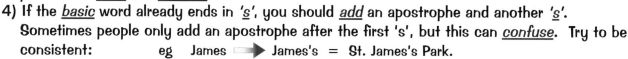

   eg The Queen ➡ The Queen's = belonging to the Queen.
       Orwell ➡ Orwell's = belonging to Orwell.

3) *Remember* — you should only use an apostrophe of possession *after* the *owner's* name.

4) If the *basic* word already ends in 's', you should *add* an apostrophe and another 's'. Sometimes people only add an apostrophe after the first 's', but this can *confuse*. Try to be consistent: eg James ➡ James's = St. James's Park.

5) If the *owner* is *plural* and the basic word ends in 's', *only* put an apostrophe after the 's':
   eg He stole the ladies' hearts with his wit and charm.   She was brave despite the tigers' roars.

6) If the *owner* is *plural* and the basic word *doesn't* end in 's', add an apostrophe *and* another 's':
   eg Estella ruined men's lives. He lifted the oxen's yoke. (men and oxen are plurals without 's')

> **IMPORTANT NOTE:** there is no apostrophe with the possessive pronouns his, hers, ours, yours or its — so don't use apostrophes with these words. The words its and it's are completely different — see below.

Apostrophes can fill in for *Missing Letters*

1) This means that the apostrophe goes *in place* of the missing letters to run two words *together* and make a *shorter* form:

   He is a brave man ➡ He's a brave man — the apostrophe *replaces* the letter '*i*'.
   I do not like you ➡ I don't like you — the apostrophe *replaces* the letter '*o*'.

2) Other *common* forms are I've, I'm, you're, they're, she's, who's (who is), I'd (I had), could've.

3) *Unusual* forms include: shall not = shan't, will not = won't, I would = I'd, let us = let's, of the clock = o'clock etc. A *special case* is the phrase 'I would have' which *could* be shortened to 'I'd've' — but *don't* try to write it, even in dialogue, because it looks far too *confusing*.

> **RULE 22:** apostrophes can be used to run two words together when letters are missed out — but never do this in essays. Use full forms for formal work.

Don't ever confuse *its* and *it's*

1) These are *different* word forms. You should *never* use '*it's*' in *formal* writing. Learn the rule:

> **RULE 23:** it's means it is or it has — nothing else. Its is like his, and shows something belongs — it shows possession and doesn't have an apostrophe.

2) *Learn* this practice phrase: I hate the apostrophe; it's had its day.
   = it has   = possession

> **RULE 24:** never use apostrophes to form ordinary plurals. Some people use apostrophes with plurals of numbers — eg 2's, 3's, 1970's. This is correct but can be confusing. It's safer not to use them for this at all.

SECTION THREE — GRAMMAR AND PUNCTUATION

Using Quotation Marks

Quotation marks or _inverted commas_ are used when someone is _speaking_ or to _quote_ from a book.

Direct Speech *is shown by* Double Quotation Marks

1) Double quotation marks are used _before_ and _after_ someone _speaks_ in a piece of writing.

2) Every time a _new person_ speaks, you must start a _new line_. The _first word_ inside the quotation mark must have a _capital letter_:

"Bet that surprised you," said Dave.

   eg "Don't go," he said. "I have to tell you something."
     "Tell me what?" asked Jane, concerned.

3) Quotation marks are _never_ used in _play_ or _film scripts_.

4) If the speech is at the _beginning_ of a sentence which _continues_ afterwards, use a _comma_ before the _final_ quotation mark: eg "Don't go," he said.

5) If the speech comes at the _end_ of a sentence, there must be a _comma_ before the _first_ quotation mark and a _full stop_ before the _final_ quotation mark: eg He said, "Please don't go."

6) The speech can also be _split in two_ for effect, and must have _commas_ before the _first_ quotation mark _and_ before the _final_ quotation mark: eg "Please," he said, "Don't go."

7) If the speech is an _exclamation_, you must use an _exclamation mark_ instead of a comma. If it is a _question_, use a _question mark_: eg "No!" screamed Tess. "Why?" asked Hamlet.

Reported Speech *Doesn't Use Quotation Marks*

1) Reported speech is when you _write_ what someone has said in _your own words_ — it's also called _indirect speech_, because the original speaker isn't talking to you directly.

2) Reported speech _never_ uses _quotation marks_; the speech is usually introduced by the word _that_.

3) If the verb in the _original direct_ speech is _present_ tense, it must change to a _past_ tense in _reported speech_. If it is _past_ tense, it becomes _pluperfect_; if it is _future_, 'will' becomes 'would'.

DIRECT SPEECH	REPORTED SPEECH
Desdemona said, "I like that fellow."	Desdemona said *that* she *liked* that fellow.
= comma before first quotation mark	= that replaces comma = past not present
"I know I've seen him before," she said.	She said *that* she knew she *had seen* him before.
= comma before last quotation mark	= pluperfect not simple past

Quotation Marks *have* Three Other Uses

1) You _must_ use quotation marks when you want to _quote_ exact words from a _book_ in an essay.

2) Use quotation marks with _titles_ of _songs_, _poems_, _essays_ or _articles_, but _not_ with the _names_ of _books_. Book titles should be _underlined_, and the _key words_ should have _capital letters_:

It's a fair cop, guv!

   eg "To be or not to be, that is the question:"
     "The Lady of Shallott"   _The Catcher in the Rye_

3) They should be used with _slang_ or _technical words_:
   eg The thief knew that the "pigs" had caught him.

IMPORTANT NOTE: single quotation marks can be used instead of doubles; but be consistent and careful — they can easily be _confused_ with apostrophes. If there are two sets of quotation marks in one sentence, you must use doubles for the _outside marks_ and singles for the _inside marks_.

Brackets, Hyphens and Dashes

Three final punctuation marks to revise here. Be especially careful not to confuse _dashes_ and _hyphens_ — they have very different jobs.

Brackets are used to Explain and Expand

1) Brackets are used to _include information_ which is not directly part of the main sentence.
2) This means that the sentence must _still_ make sense _without_ the phrase in brackets — _remember_ the rule:

RULE 25: brackets always come in pairs; at the beginning and the end of a phrase which explains or expands on the main sentence.

   eg They were determined to find the ship (it was full of silver).

3) If the brackets come at the _end_ of the main sentence (as above) then there must be a _full stop outside_ the end bracket.
4) If there is a _complete_ sentence _inside_ the brackets and it comes between _two other_ sentences, then there should be a _full stop inside_ the end bracket:

   eg He had spent years looking for the ship. (It had sunk in the area many years before.) At last his search was over.

Don't confuse Hyphens with Dashes

RULE 26: hyphens are symbols used to join words or parts of words — dashes are used to separate one part of a sentence from another.

Dashes can be used Singly or in Pairs

1) Dashes look like this: — . A dash must always have a _space_ before and after it.
2) _Pairs_ of dashes are used in the _same_ way as _brackets_; they _separate_ a phrase which explains what went before, but _only_ in the _middle_ of a sentence:

   eg The ship suddenly struck the rocks — the lookout had fallen asleep — and it slowly began to sink.

3) _Never_ use pairs of dashes at the _end_ of a sentence.
4) A _single_ dash can be used instead of a _colon_ — this sentence is a good example.
5) It can also _link_ two clauses that wouldn't be sentences by themselves, especially in _headings_ or _titles:_   eg The internet — the future of education.

Hyphens have Three Main Uses

1) Hyphens are used to _join_ words that are part of the _same idea_ to make them _one word_, and with _numbers:_ eg gold-rimmed, up-to-date, free-for-all, duck-billed, eighty-two, twenty-one.
2) These are usually _adjective_ phrases, and the separate words form part of _one main idea:_
   eg "a free-swimming duck," means something different from "a free swimming duck".
3) Hyphens are also used to join _prefixes_ to words. These are fixed to the _beginning_ of words to _change_ the _meaning:_ eg _anti-_ anti-drugs, _re-_ re-record, _de-_ de-icer, _co-_ co-write.
4) Hyphens help to make words _easier to read_, and help avoid _confusing_ two possible meanings:

eg   sword-dance,   de-icer,   fifty-odd people,   he resigned but later re-signed.

clearer than deicer

two 'd's = hard to read   **fifty odd people means something else**   **these are opposites**

<u>*Negatives*</u>

Negatives are simple to form in English, but there are two very <u>common mistakes</u> that you must make sure you <u>avoid</u>: mistakes with <u>double negatives</u> and mistakes with the word <u>none</u>.

<u>*Don't use Double Negatives*</u>

1) A <u>negative</u> sentence is where you want to say <u>'no'</u> or <u>'not'</u> — the opposite of a positive:

    eg   I like everyone in this room = <u>positive</u>

2) <u>One way</u> to make this sentence <u>negative</u> is using a negative form of the verb <u>to do</u> = <u>do not</u>.

3) We also need to change the word <u>'everyone'</u> to the word <u>'anyone'</u>.

4) Alternatively we could keep the <u>same verb</u> and <u>change</u> the word <u>everyone</u> to <u>no-one</u>.

5) The negative sentences are: I do not like anyone in this room <u>or</u> I like no-one in this room.

6) Some people try to give more <u>emphasis</u> by using <u>more than one</u> negative word. This is often because they <u>confuse</u> the two forms of the negative: eg I do not like no-one in this room.

7) In this case there are <u>two</u> negatives — so they <u>cancel</u> each other out: I do not like no-one actually means 'I do not not like anyone', which means 'I like everyone'. <u>Learn</u> the rule:

> **<u>RULE 27:</u> two negative words in the same phrase will make it positive; you should only use one negative at a time.**

      eg   I don't want anything <u>or</u> I want nothing   (I don't want nothing = <u>WRONG</u>)

8) The set phrase 'neither...nor' is <u>not</u> a double negative — it is used to talk about more than one object in the sentence, not with the verb.

      eg I haven't seen either Malcolm or MacDuff   <u>or</u>   I have seen neither Malcolm nor MacDuff.

<u>*The Word None has Three Meanings*</u>

<u>OBJECT (P. 19)</u>

1) None is a word that can cause <u>problems</u>. As a <u>pronoun</u> it means <u>'not one'</u> or <u>'not any'</u>:

    eg   — Did you see any film stars?   <u>or</u>   — Have you got any trip hop CDs?
         — We saw <u>none</u>.   — I'm afraid there are <u>none</u> left.

2) As an <u>adverb</u>, none means <u>'not at all'</u>:

    eg   Surprisingly, the fish were <u>none</u> the worse for living in a different kettle.

3) None should <u>not</u> be used with <u>other</u> negative words (see double negative rule):

    eg   He has none (He's not got none = <u>WRONG</u>). We saw none (We didn't see none = <u>WRONG</u>).

<u>*The Word Ain't is Never Used in Formal English*</u>

1) Lots of people use the word <u>'ain't'</u> when they speak: eg "She ain't got any." "I ain't been there."

2) This <u>doesn't exist</u> in formal English, and you will <u>lose marks</u> if you use it in your <u>Exam</u> work.

3) The <u>standard</u> form is <u>'hasn't'</u> or <u>'haven't'</u>, or part of the verb <u>'to be'</u>, but <u>remember</u> that you <u>don't</u> use apostrophes in formal <u>essay</u> work. You must write <u>'has not'</u> or <u>'have not'</u>.

4) <u>Don't forget</u> the double negative rule: eg   He hasn't got none = <u>WRONG</u>. He has none = <u>FINE</u>.

<u>*The Key Words we haven't covered — 'a'/'an' and 'the'*</u>

1) The words <u>'a'</u> and <u>'the'</u> are called <u>articles</u>; <u>'the'</u> is the <u>definite</u> article, 'a' is the <u>indefinite</u>.

> **<u>RULE 28:</u> the is the definite article, used for something you definitely mean; a is the indefinite article, used when you don't have anything specific in mind.**

      eg   <u>the</u> car = specific car,   <u>a</u> car = any car, not a specific one.

2) The word <u>'a'</u> is used with <u>all</u> nouns <u>except</u> those beginning with the letter <u>'h'</u> and all <u>vowels</u> — a, e, i, o, u. These words take <u>'an'</u> instead: eg <u>an</u> orange, <u>an</u> undertaker, <u>an</u> hotel.

3) <u>Don't forget</u> that words with <u>'h'</u> take <u>'an'</u> — people often get this wrong: eg <u>an</u> hospital.

Sentences and Word Order

A _sentence_ is a _group of words_ which makes total sense _on its own_. The keys to writing _good_ sentences are making sure that _subject_, _verb_ and _tense agree_, and using the right _word order_.

The Subject and Verb must agree

1) This is really _very easy_. When the _subject_ is _singular_, the _verb_ must be _singular_; when the _subject_ is _plural_, then so is the _verb_. Follow the rule:

> **RULE 29:** look at what you want to say and ask who or what performed the action. This is the subject, and the verb must agree with it.

    eg The sword is poisoned = _singular_ subject and verb.   These swords are poisoned = _plural_.

2) Things can become _complicated_ when the _subject_ is a _group_ of words: eg a sack of potatoes. Just remember the rule — ask yourself whether the subject is '_sack_' or '_potatoes_', and make the _verb_ agree: eg A _sack_ of potatoes only _costs_ five pounds.

       | singular subject | | singular verb |

3) If there is _more_ than one _subject_, linked by the word '_and_', then the _verb_ is _plural_, even if _both_ individual subject nouns are _singular_: eg Romeo _and_ Juliet _are_ happy.

4) If there is _more_ than one _verb_, then remember the rule and look at the _subject_:

    eg This new recipe _looks_ delicious but _tastes_ like elephant dung. (recipe is a singular subject)

Learn these Special Words with Special Agreement Rules

1) Everyone, someone, anyone, no-one, and each	= SINGULAR subjects ➤	SINGULAR verbs
2) Many, both, few and several	= PLURAL subjects ➤	PLURAL verbs
3) Collective nouns, such as team, class, and family	= SINGULAR subjects ➤	SINGULAR verbs
4) Neither...nor... ➤	If both subjects are SINGULAR, use a SINGULAR verb	
	➤ If both subjects are PLURAL, use a PLURAL verb	

Sentences also depend on Clear Word Order

1) Many sentences will _change in meaning_ if you alter the _word order_.

> I just told Chris that the ferret bit me (= I told _Chris recently_).
> I told just Chris that the ferret bit me (= I told _only Chris_).
> I told Chris just that the ferret bit me (= I told Chris _only the fact_ that it bit me).
> I told Chris that the ferret just bit me (= I told Chris that _it bit me recently_).

2) Think what you _want_ to say, and whether you are really saying what you _mean_.

3) Verbs ending in _-ing_ or _-ed_ must be _close_ to the _subject_ they relate to:

    eg I saw some snails walking in the park   Walking in the park, I saw some snails
          = the snails were walking   = I was walking

4) _Avoid_ sub-clauses separating subjects from their verbs — they are _hard_ to follow:

    eg Polonius, hiding behind the arras while Hamlet spoke to the Queen, held his breath.
          = _clumsy_ to read, so the _subject_ Polonius should go _with_ the verb.

        Hiding behind the arras, Polonius held his breath while Hamlet spoke to the Queen.

Avoid Split Infinitives — They will Lose you Marks

1) _Infinitives_ are made of the word '_to_' + _the basic form of the verb_ (see also P.15 and P.23).

2) _Split infinitives_ arise when the '_to_' and the _other_ word are _separated_, often by an adverb:

    eg to boldly go, to carefully look = these forms are considered _incorrect_ and will _lose marks_.

3) Instead you should _keep_ the _two parts_ of the verb _together_: eg to go boldly, to look carefully.

Sentences and Paragraphs

Time for a few *tips* on how to put words *together* — you should also look at P.71 on writing skills.

Use Sentences Carefully

1) Sentences can be used to *state facts*, to *ask questions*, to *make exclamations* or to *give commands*. They can contain several *clauses* or only one.
2) Each sentence should contain *one main idea* — no more: eg Let's go racing! Did you like it?
3) All *new* sentences should *begin* with a *capital letter* and *end* with a *full stop*, *exclamation mark* or *question mark*.

Paragraphs are Groups of Sentences

My paragraph was this big!

1) A paragraph is a *group of sentences* about a *related topic*. They are used to break a piece of writing into *sections*, making it *easier to read* (see also P.71 on writing skills).
2) A paragraph is *shown* on the page by setting the *first line* in from the margin — when you write by hand, try to leave the same *gap* as the word *'space'* would take up.
3) Paragraphs can be *any length* — but you should *avoid* very *short* or very *long* paragraphs. *Don't forget* the rule:

> **RULE 30:** if the sentence you want to write is closely related to the last one you wrote, put it in the same paragraph. If you are talking about a different idea or topic, start a new paragraph. Make sure your paragraphs aren't too long.

Example of Paragraphs in an Essay

one main idea leading on from the last sentence

space

one main idea in the sentence

When Cordelia refuses to speak, she defies her father. Saying that she loves Lear in a long and exaggerated speech, as Goneril and Regan did, does not prove anything. Cordelia believes that genuine love cannot be measured. Even though she loves her father, she will not do what he wants. This is what real love is in *King Lear*.

In the same way, Kent is the only person present who is prepared to stand up against the King. When Lear grows angry with Cordelia, Kent is prepared to tell him he is in the wrong: "be Kent unmannerly / When Lear is mad."

By speaking out, however, Kent is being disloyal to his feudal lord. When he tells Lear that he is wrong, Kent is defying the whole system of loyalty that says the King has absolute power, and his subjects must do as they are told. Just as Cordelia defies the traditional system of family loyalty, Kent defies the traditional system of loyalty to the King.

margin

paragraph not too long

Remember to Watch your Tenses

1) If you *start* an essay or a piece of creative writing in one *tense*, make sure you *stay* in the *same* tense. If you *start* in the *past*, *stay* in the *past*. Don't change tense.
2) Be careful with *similar-sounding* forms. Think what you *want* to say:

I was *eating*
= I did the eating

I was *eaten*
= something else ate me

Revision Summary for Section Three

Thirty rules for you to learn here — but they're all directly relevant to your writing style. If you learn them, you will avoid making the basic mistakes in grammar and punctuation that lose marks in written or oral work. This will automatically improve your chances of doing well.

These rules will also help you to start noticing how other writers use language — we'll look at this in detail in Sections Five and Six. Before that, you need to practise what you've learned. If you can learn all the rules, your writing will definitely be clearer to read and understand. Try to answer these questions without looking back; see how much you've learned. Don't forget; if there's something you're still unsure about, go back through the Section and revise it again.

1) What's wrong with saying 'They should of called me'? What should the sentence say?
2) When do you use 'would' and when do you use 'should'? Give two examples using each word.
3) Explain the difference between 'Can I come in?' and 'May I come in?'
4) What is a noun and what is a pronoun?
5) What's the difference between a subject pronoun and an object pronoun?
6) What is an adjective? What is an adverb? Give three sentences using adjectives and adverbs.
7) How would you explain what a conjunction is?
8) What's the rule about using 'and' or 'but' at the start of a sentence?
9) What does a preposition do in a sentence?
10) What sort of pronoun must always go after a preposition?
11) 'Different to', 'different than' or 'different from': which is the form you should use and why?
12) Why shouldn't you use the phrase 'between...or....?' What should you say instead?
13) 'Brutus was greatly effected by the death of Portia.' What's wrong with this sentence?
14) Why shouldn't you ask someone if they will borrow you their book?
15) Stationary and stationery; which goes with pens and which with cars?
16) What's the difference between to, two and too?
17) When would you use 'practice' and when would you use 'practise'? Give examples.
18) What is a dependent clause?
19) Which punctuation mark is used to link two sentences that are equally important? There are two possible answers. Give an example using one.
20) Which puntuation mark is used to link two sentences where one explains the other?
21) What's the difference between it's and its? Write three sentences using them.
22) What's the problem with writing 'Carrot's 16p per pound'?
23) What is a double negative? Why should you avoid using them?
24) What do the subject and the verb in a sentence do?
25) Correct these sentences:
   I been to the chip van, I got two special burger's for me and Steve.
   The van was stationery; the car just drove straight into it.
   If he'd known the film was on he could of gone and seen it.
   I done the shopping yesterday.
26) Write a mini-essay on "Three Grammar Rules which I find difficult." Explain each of the rules and why you find them hard. Practise writing clear paragraphs and sentences.
27) What is grammar? What is the key to learning grammar?
28) What is punctuation? Why is it important?
29) Write two sentences using question marks, and then re-write them as indirect questions. Don't forget that indirect questions don't have question marks.
30) Explain the difference between direct speech and reported speech. Re-write these sentences as reported speech:
   "We shall never surrender," said the Anglo-Saxon Commander.   "Let me go!" yelled Mina.

Reading for a Reason

Comprehension means looking for clues in a text to help you understand it and to help you answer questions on it. _Remember_ — the more you practise reading, the better your _marks_ will get.

Three Reasons why Reading is the Key to Good Marks

1) Reading _carefully_ means that you _notice things_ when you read — the way a character is described, or a line of poetry that sticks in your mind. Noting down these details will help you to _write well_ about your reading in essay work and in your Exams.
2) Reading _widely_ helps you to see _links_ between writers and texts and to _compare_ them — eg the different views of the future in Orwell's _Nineteen Eighty-four_, and Huxley's _Brave New World_.
3) Reading helps you to spot the little _tricks_ writers use to create a _reaction_ in the reader. This will help you to write about their _use of language_. You can also start _using_ these tricks to improve your _own_ writing (see Section Five, P.42-52).

Any Kind of Reading will Improve your Marks

1) You will have to read some _specific_ books for your Exams and Coursework — but if you read _other_ things too, you'll be _improving_ your ability to read carefully and _notice_ things.
2) _Any_ piece of writing can be read and studied — whether it's a _novel_, a _poem_ or a _diary_. When you talk about pieces of writing in this way, they are called _texts_.
3) You can also read _newspaper_ or _magazine_ articles, _short stories_ and even some _graphic novels_. The best way to improve your reading is to read a _variety_ of different types of text.
4) Anything that you _enjoy_ reading will help you to _practise_ the main skills in this section — the skills of _comprehension_, also known as _practical criticism_.

> **REMEMBER**: comprehension is about how clearly you understand a piece of text — and also about whether you can read between the lines.

Learn to Read Between the Lines

1) Writers _don't_ always say exactly what they _mean_ when they write.
2) Reading between the lines means learning to look for _hidden meanings_ in a text.
3) Hidden meanings can take many forms. _Characters_ may be _lying_ to the reader, or _joking_, or even being _deliberately boring_.
4) Sometimes the _narrator_ of a text may _exaggerate_ or say something which is _obviously untrue_ — to be funny, perhaps:

> eg   It is a truth universally acknowledged, that a single man in possession of a fortune must be in want of a wife.
> (_Pride and Prejudice_, Chapter 1; Jane Austen)

These hidden meanings are part of the writer's _style_ — you need to learn how to _spot them_.

Reading — I thought that was in Berkshire...

We're going to focus on _practical criticism skills_ in this Section. This means reading in _detail_ and _summarising_ what you've read so that you can _answer questions_ or _write essays_ about it. These are the basics of _comprehension_ — you'll need them for _fiction_ and _non-fiction_ texts.

Scanning and Close Reading

Comprehension is tested in the Exam and in Coursework exercises, using short *extracts* from texts. You'll have to recognise all the *main details* of the extract in a *limited* period of time.

Scanning means Reading for the Main Ideas

1) Start by reading the extract through *quickly*.
2) You're *not* trying to understand *every detail*; just the *main ideas* in the text.
3) Note down any *key points*, and *underline* any sentences and ideas you *weren't sure* about. You can look at them again later. Don't spend too long scanning — read it as *quickly* as you can.

For example:

If you're reading a passage describing a room, you should scan the text for the basic details. Look for the main features of the room — some kind of general description; perhaps it has bare walls, a little, barred window and straw on the floor.

Close Reading means Looking for the Details

1) Go over the text *in detail* before you start writing about it.
2) Read each sentence *carefully*, making sure you *understand* it. If you don't, then read the last sentence *again* — then read the problem sentence through *slowly*, until you understand it.
3) When you've read the whole thing through, look at the *beginning* and the *end*. If the text is an extract from a longer text, you *won't* have all of the argument — look *only* at what *you have*.
4) Look at any *questions* you are asked about the text. These are the things the Examiners *want you* to notice — so make sure you look out for them.
5) Then go through the text *again*, taking *clear notes* of the points which are relevant to *answering* the questions. Be careful not to miss anything.

REMEMBER — you're *only* being tested on the *passage in front of you*; that's ALL you should write about. *Don't* add information *unless* the question asks for it.

For example:

After close reading of the text describing the room, you should be able to give a lot more detail — there is a skeleton in chains in the corner, a bed on the left and a rat asleep in the straw.

Scanning and re-reading — getting close to a text...

Reading the text through twice *seems* like twice as much work — but you'll *miss out* on a lot of detail if you don't. If you're asked to *compare* two texts, scan and close read *each* text by *itself* then read them one after the other to look for *similarities* and *differences*. Try a scan read and a close read of *this page* to find out the six main points — it's the only way to practise.

Making a Summary

A clear, accurate summary only gives the _vital information_ from a text. Any extra, irrelevant details are _left out_. Summarising will seriously improve your quick reading skills — so learn _how_ to do it.

Firstly, Work Out What is Relevant

1) You _can't summarise_ if you _haven't read_ the text carefully.
2) Start by _scanning_ the text, then reading it _closely_.
3) Once you understand the _whole text_, go through it again _slowly_, working out what's _relevant_, and which details can be _left out_.
4) Write _only_ the number of words you're allowed — _no more_.
5) See what the _title_ is, and look for any extra information on the paper which could be relevant, like the author's name.
6) Decide what the _main theme_ of the text is.

I've only read the first page and I allready know who the murderer is!

Rubbish Holmes!

Make Sure Your Summary is the Right Length

1) If the question says _how many words_ long the summary must be, you must _never_ write _more_ than that limit. You will definitely _lose marks_ if you don't follow the guidelines.
2) Make sure that _all_ the _basic information_ is there — _don't_ include detail when there isn't room.

Look at the example article below, and the 50 word summary which follows it:

Always Bank on a Toad — Pet Ends Hostage Crisis

Animal-loving hero Dave Roe, 47, and his brave pet toad Miguel, 3, were this evening recovering at home after being held hostage at gunpoint during a dramatic hour-long ordeal at the East Road Branch of the Renton Hill Bank. Mr. Roe was signing a form when three masked men with shotguns entered the Bank and demanded one thousand pounds in cash.

"The cashier was too scared to move," said Mr. Roe, during an exclusive interview with our correspondent. "One bloke threatened her. His mate put a gun to my head. He said he'd shoot if they didn't get the money. Just my luck! I only went in to borrow a fiver."

Assistant Manager Bryan Pickets quickly handed over the cash, and the criminals made their escape, taking the terrified but defiant Mr. Roe as a hostage. The desperate gang escaped with the loot in a green sports car waiting outside, driven by another masked scoundrel.

The crooks hadn't counted on Amazonian Attack Toad, Miguel, however. Arriving at the thieves' hideout, Miguel leapt from the hole in owner Roe's pocket, breaking the wrist of one cowardly robber. As the surprised villain dropped his gun, Miguel cornered the other two with his poisonous tongue. The plucky toad kept all three would-be bandits from escaping until police arrived. "It just shows you should always keep a toad in the hole," Mr. Roe said.

The Renton Hill Bank on East Road was robbed at gunpoint today by three masked men and an accomplice in a green sports car. They escaped with one thousand pounds cash and a hostage, customer Dave Roe, but were later arrested after Mr. Roe's pet toad Miguel had disarmed them.

Accurate information is rewarded — summary justice...

Remember, writing a summary means keeping the _important_ points and _nothing else_. You won't be able to write an accurate summary if you haven't _read_ the text through _properly_ first.

How To Take Notes

Taking notes when you read is the _easiest way_ to summarize — it's a key comprehension skill.

Be Clear and Concise — Don't Just Repeat Everything

1) Taking notes is the _first step_ to sorting through a text. You're looking for _key information_ — nothing else. Any other information in the text may be _misleading_ at this stage.
2) Notes _don't_ have to be full sentences — they can just be _key words_ or _abbreviations_. It doesn't matter if other people can't read them; just make sure _you_ can understand them.

An Example of Note-Taking:

> Plymouth-based divers have spent the last three months searching for the legendary lost treasure of the Guadeloupe. This Spanish Galleon disappeared in 1804, when she is believed to have sunk with the loss of all hands. At the time it was rumoured that the ship was carrying silver plate from Mexico, but no trace of the wreck or the treasure has ever been found.
>
> Earlier this year, however, a Princeton University Historian claimed to have discovered the site of the wreck. After preliminary dives by a local expert, the presence of several mysterious objects on the sea-bed was confirmed. Unfortunately, bad weather prevented further exploration for a whole frustrating month.
>
> Since then, the area has been full of divers, but no-one found any sign of either the wreck or the treasure until yesterday, when a diver claimed to have discovered the strange objects again.
>
> They were carefully raised, only to be identified as beer barrels. It is believed that there are approximately 45 barrels, but it is unclear how they ended up in at the bottom of the sea. The salvage team now has plans to record a single for charity. The song: "Roll out the Barrel".

Brief notes only include the key words — you can expand your notes later if you need to:
Treasure Hunt, shipwreck — Guadeloupe 1804, rumour of lost silver, historian claimed to find site, divers searched, objects seen, three months later objects found to be 45-odd beer barrels.

REMEMBER: you write notes to help you understand the text; not instead of the text. If you're in doubt, or you left something out, always go back to the text.

1) If you're asked about something that _doesn't_ appear in your notes, go back to the _text_ again.
2) Your notes are there to help you find information _quickly_; they _don't_ have to be perfect, but you'll find it easier to answer questions quickly if your notes are as _accurate_ as possible.

Draft Your Notes into a Rough Copy

1) In a _comprehension_ exercise you'll be given questions to answer or an essay to write, based on the text. To pick up _high marks_, your final answer must be _clear_ and _organised_.
2) A rough copy is a _rough version_ of your _answer_, using the information in your notes. This _doesn't_ have to be _neat_ or totally _accurate_. It should be a _practice_ version of your final answer.
3) When you have a rough copy, go _back over_ the text and see if you have _missed out_ any information relevant to the question, or _added_ anything _irrelevant_.
4) Then check your _grammar_ and your _sentences_. Make sure your final version is in _clear_, _accurate_, _neatly-written_, _standard_ English.
5) _Don't_ spend too long on notes or rough copies. Use them to _improve_ your _final version_ — this will improve the _mark_ you get for the exercise. It's like a make-over — before and after.

SECTION FOUR — COMPREHENSION

Putting Comprehension Skills Together

Learn how to recognise the different styles of questions you may be given, and the kind of answers the Examiners will be looking for.

Start by Scanning the Passage

1) Scan the passage quickly for the overall meaning. If something is confusing, go over it until it becomes clear.
2) REMEMBER — you are only looking for a rough picture.

Read the Passage Closely to Understand the Detail

1) Close reading is about detail — but only relevant detail.
2) As you read the text closely, underline key words and phrases, and take notes of the main points in the piece.
3) Go back over the text to check you haven't missed anything.
4) Look out for hidden meanings: whether the writer is saying what they mean, whether the writer is talking in the voice of a character or a biased observer (see P.43).

Answer only the questions you're asked; give the exact answer required for each.

Different Kinds of Question Require Different Answers

> The circus suddenly exploded into life in front of Jane. Everywhere she saw bright, whirling lights and flashing colours. She shivered in excitement.
> Jane and her aunt paused in front of the ticket kiosk. Aunt Matilda patted her coat pockets absently as she tried to find the tickets. Her arthritis made simple tasks so difficult now.
> "Now, what did I do with those tickets?" Aunt Matilda saw Jane's worried look.
> "Don't worry, dear," she said. "I'll soon find them and then we'll be in. Just you wait! When I was your age, I used to love the circus — especially the clowns! Now where are those tickets?"

1) LITERAL QUESTIONS — ask you to find out information plainly written in the text:
 eg Which parts of the passage suggest to you that Aunt Matilda is old?

1) Decide what the question is asking you, then look through the text to find any relevant parts.
2) Check again to ensure you haven't missed anything: eg She has arthritis, she can't remember where she put the tickets, she talks about what she used to do when she was young.
3) Write a rough answer to the question; check it and write a neat final copy.

2) CLOSE READING QUESTIONS — ask you to look closely at the text to give opinions.
 eg What sort of character do you think Aunt Matilda has? Use the information in the passage.

1) Work out exactly what the question is asking you. Look for hidden meanings in the text.
2) Go through the text looking for relevant information: eg She is absent-minded because she can't find the tickets, she is kind and observant because she notices Jane is worried.
3) Take notes and write a rough answer to the question, putting your best point first. If you quote from the text, remember the rules (P.29). Check your grammar and write a final neat copy.
4) NEVER make up information or add anything that doesn't appear in the text given to you.

3) PERSONAL QUESTIONS — ask you to write about your own ideas or experiences:
 eg   What do you think of circuses? Give reasons for and against them.

Answering the Question

The secret to _good marks_ in comprehension exercises is to make sure you _answer the question_. That means looking _carefully_ at what it _means_ and how many _marks_ it is worth.

Answer Only the Questions You Have Been Asked

1) It sounds obvious, but many people don't _read_ the questions _properly_. Take your time to work out _exactly_ what is asked.
2) Ask yourself what _kind_ of question it is: a _literal_ question, or a _close reading_ question or a _personal writing_ question.

eg — How does John change by the end of the story from what he is like at the beginning? = CLOSE READING QUESTION.

— "People are not only educated in the classroom." To what extent is this statement true? = PERSONAL QUESTION.

REMEMBER: you're being examined on how carefully you read the questions as well as how carefully you read the text. Read the questions through first.

Give Only Enough Detail to Pick Up All the Marks

1) Every question should have a _number_ beside it, showing how many _marks_ the question is worth.
2) This tells you _how detailed_ your answer has to be, and how much _time_ to give it in an Exam.
3) If a question is worth _twenty marks_, you'll need to give a _lot_ of _detail_ for the marks.
4) If a question is worth _five marks_, then don't _waste_ time giving _extra_ information. Even if you write the greatest answer ever, you _won't_ get any _more_ than five marks for it!

Look at the Example:

Harry Flash clung desperately to the monkey-puzzle tree. He didn't dare look, but he could feel the hot breath of the lion's mouth against his ankles. The lion roared, and Harry wondered uneasily how safe he was in the tree. His water bottle still hung over one arm, and the bag of mint humbugs his mother had sent from England hung over the other. His gun lay by the lion.

Bad luck old chap

QUESTION: Where was Harry Flash and why? (2)
Answer 1: Harry Flash was trapped in a monkey-puzzle tree. He had been chased there by a lion which was still waiting underneath, preventing him from escaping.
Answer 2: Harry Flash was clinging to a tree, with a bag of mint humbugs and a water bottle. His gun was beside the lion which had chased him into the tree, and he was worried in case the lion could climb trees. He'd had better Christmas Days.

1) The first answer is _better_ because it answers the question in _detail_, and _only_ gives the _relevant_ facts. The question is worth _two marks_, and the answer makes _two points_ — _where_ Harry is and _why_ he is there. The answer _only_ uses information from the text.
2) The second answer gives lots of _irrelevant_ information. It starts off well, by saying _where_ Harry Flash is, but then talks about what he is _holding_, which is _not_ asked for in the question. This answer also _adds_ information which _isn't_ in the text — _never_ do this in your work.

Answer the question you're given — simple enough...

You must read the question properly. You'll win marks for _picking out_ bits of the text that are _relevant_ to the question and for _using_ them in your answer. If you've read the question _wrongly_ then you'll be looking for the _wrong_ things in the text — that _isn't_ going to get you the marks. If your notes haven't got the information you need, then look at the _text_ again. Keep _practising_.

Revision Summary for Section Four

Comprehension is the set of basic skills used for reading any text, whether it's fiction, journalism or poetry. Your school may call it practical criticism, but the idea is the same. It's about how you look at a text to find out what it says on the surface, and what may be hidden underneath.

Remember also that some comprehension questions in the Exam will be marked for your reading skills, and some will be marked for writing. The writing skills will be tested by personal questions, asking you to write your own ideas in response to the text. Reading questions will ask you to look closely at the text and use only the information you find in it, unless the question itself says otherwise. Most extracts will be between two or three pages — poems will usually be shorter.

1) What are the three reasons why reading is the key to good marks?
2) What are pieces of writing called when you study them?
3) What do you look for when you read between the lines?
4) What four things should you do before you start to answer a Reading question?
5) Why do you need to read the text twice?
6) How should your second reading be different from your first reading?
7) What should you do if you don't understand a sentence when you're reading?
8) How long should a summary be?
9) What should a summary include, and what should it leave out?
10) Why is it important to make a set of notes as you read through the text?
11) What should you do if the answer isn't in your notes?
12) What are the three main sorts of question you could be asked in a comprehension exercise?
13) What do literal questions need you to do?
14) What should you do if you're asked to give your opinion of a character in the text?
15) What's the secret to good marks in comprehension questions?
16) Do you need to give all the main points of the text in your answer?
17) Why is it important to look at the number of marks a question is worth?
18) What should you never do in your answers?
19) Look at this extract from a poem and answer the comprehension questions:

I remember, I remember,
The house where I was born,
The little window where the sun
Came peeping in at morn;
He never came a wink too soon,
Nor brought too long a day,
But now I often wish the night
Had borne my breath away.

I remember, I remember,
The roses, red and white,
The violets, and the lily-cups,
Those flowers made of light!
The lilacs where the robin built,
And where my brother set
The laburnum on his birthday,—
The tree is living yet!
(from "I Remember, I Remember," by Thomas Hood)

a) What is the poet describing in the extract?
b) What is the tone he uses? How do the descriptions he gives make you feel?
c) How does he describe the sun? What does he say it used to do in the morning?
d) How does the tone change in the seventh line? What is the tone when the poet talks about the past? What is the tone when he talks about "now"?
e) How do the rhymes of the poem affect the tone?
f) Why do you think the poet remembers only beautiful things about the past?
g) Write a short account of something you remember from when you were younger. Try to describe it clearly.

Looking at Literature

Literature actually means any _written text_. This section is about _fictional_ literary texts — _poems_, _novels_ and _plays_ — and the _techniques_ to use when you read them.

Reading Literature Carefully Will Win You High Marks

1) This Section concentrates on _reading_ literature, not on writing about it.
2) Your _comprehension skills_ will be useful here; you will need to be able to _scan_, _read closely_ and take clear and accurate _notes_ from any text you study.
3) _Remember;_ language is a _tool_. Authors don't just use it to tell stories, but to make _characters_ come _alive_, to make you feel different _emotions_ and to make you _react_ in certain ways to characters and events.
4) Your job is to learn to spot _how_ a text is creating these reactions, and what _tricks_ the writer is using.
5) Any piece of writing uses tricks to make you react a certain way — in the same way a car advertisement is written to _influence you_ to buy that make of car.

Can't read, eh?

> Literary texts are written to achieve effects, and they use many tricks to create them. You need to learn what the tricks are, and how to spot them.

Different Styles Can Create Certain Effects

The _style_ of a text should tell you what _effect_ the author wants. Style is part of _any_ kind of text. It can be divided up into _three key features_.

1) _THE LANGUAGE USED:_ the language could be _formal_ or _informal_; it may be written like _speech_, or just _descriptive_. The sentences could be _short_, like those of a child, or _long_ and rambling like an older person looking back on their life. The text may be in _dialect_, like a book by Walter Scott or Irvine Welsh. It might contain _dialogue_ or none at all. It may use lots of _imagery_.

2) _THE VOCABULARY USED:_ the vocabulary could be very _simple_, as though it was spoken by a child or a mentally-handicapped person. It could be _complicated_ and full of _technical terms_, such as legal or medical terms. It could _repeat itself_ to emphasise points.

3) _THE TONE:_ the tone is the way in which the words used _create a feeling_ about what is happening; a horror story uses images of darkness, shadows and gloom — nothing is ever clear. _Wuthering Heights_ uses the images of the landscape and the weather to represent the emotions of the characters. Tennyson's poems often create a sense of imprisonment and stillness.

The style of a _description_ can completely _change_ how we see a situation or a character. Look at these two descriptions of Ms. Tique:

Ms. Tique was on the phone.
"You're late!" she growled at him. "What time do you call this?"
"I was held up," Dave replied, with a smile.
"What kind of an excuse is that?" Ms. Tique looked annoyed.
"The bank I was in...It was held up."

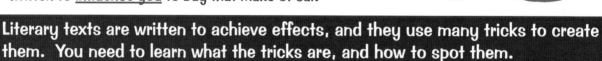

Ms. Tique laughed at his joke and winked at him across the table.
"Call me Susanna!" she whispered breathlessly.
Dave swallowed nervously. He had never met anyone as charming.
"Shall we go dancing later?" Susanna raised an eyebrow inquisitively.
She leaned forward and touched his hand.
"Aaarrg!" said Dave. It was all he could think of to say.

Understanding the Text

Many people _only_ remember the parts of a text they liked; you need to read it _more closely_, so that you can _write_ about it and _answer questions_ on it. That means you need to know _what to look for_.

The Deadly Half-Dozen — the Six Major Questions

There are _six questions_ you need to ask about any text: _who_, _what_, _where_, _when_, _how_ and _why_. Answering these questions will tell you _all the basics_.

1) Find Out Who Appears in the Text, and Who is Narrating

1) Look at the _characters_ who appear, and how they are _described_. Take _notes_ on each character to help you remember _who_ they are and _what they do_ and _say_.
2) In a _play_, the stage directions tell you who says what.
3) _Poems_, _novels_ and _short stories_ will have a _narrator_.
4) All narrators are _biased_ when they tell a story; they may be _lying_ or changing the _facts_. The text will give you _clues_ if this is happening — there may be _contradictions_ (see P.68).

It really suits you, honest

WARNING: _don't_ confuse the _author_ with the _narrator_. The author is the _real person_ who _wrote_ the text; the narrator is a _voice_ created to _talk_ to the reader.

Narrators and Authors — Look Who's Talking

1) _All_ texts have a _narrative voice_ — the voice that talks to the reader.
2) This voice may be a _character_ in the text, or an _observer_. Some narrators are _biased_, and give their _opinions_ on events. Others don't _comment_ on what happens; they just _report_ it.
3) Even when the text addresses the reader _directly_, the voice that is speaking is a _narrator_.
4) Whenever authors write they use different _styles_ of narrative voice to create different _effects_.
5) In the course of a _novel_, an author may use _many_ narrative voices; sometimes the narrator may know everything (_omniscience_), or the narrator may be in more than one place (_omnipresence_).
6) Don't forget — _never_ confuse authors with narrators.

2) Find Out What Happens, and What Each Character Does

1) Make a _list_ of the _characters_ and _what they do_ in the course of the text.
2) Then make a list of _anything else_ that happens. Look out for _accidents_, _natural disasters_ and even the _weather_. They are often used to create the atmosphere of a text.
3) You can even do this for _poems_ — just work out all the events and actions which take place. Make a list of the details so you don't forget.
4) Note down any points when characters _fail_ to do something: for example in Shakespeare's _King Lear_, _Edmund_ fails to send a _message_ in time to save _Cordelia's_ life.
5) If you don't understand any of the _vocabulary_ in a text, _look up_ what it means.

REMEMBER: _no_ event in a literary text is really an accident — there's always a _reason_ why the author included it, even if it's only for atmosphere or style.

Who and What — a test of character

Plenty to revise here. Start by learning the _six major questions_ — they're useful for looking at _any text_, and for _writing reports_ (see P.92). Remember the _difference_ between _narrators_ and _authors_.

Where, When, How and Why

Every time you look at a text, _ask_ these questions and _note down_ your answers. _Make sure_ you learn them thoroughly.

3) Look at Where the Action Takes Place

1) The _setting_ of a text is _always_ important. Even if it doesn't _seem_ relevant, you _should_ try to find it out.
2) Some texts are _deliberately_ set in _one place_, such as Samuel Beckett's play _Waiting for Godot_, or Tennyson's poem "Mariana," both about waiting. Others are set in _several places_: Oscar Wilde's _The Importance of Being Earnest_ moves between town and country.

4) When the Action Happens / When the Narrator is Speaking

1) You need to know _when_ the events of a text take place. This will help you to see the _structure_ of the text — the _reason_ things happen in a certain order.
2) Some texts cover a period of _many years_, like _Wuthering Heights_. Others cover a _short_ period of time — many poems try to capture _one moment_ in time.
3) Narrators can be immediate _eyewitnesses_, or they may be looking back on the _past_.
4) Some texts present _two views_ of events; an _eyewitness_ version, and a _second_ version, reflecting on the same events _much later_. This happens in _Great Expectations_, where the narrator, _Pip_, sometimes speaks and acts like a _child_, and sometimes like a mature _adult_.

5) How the Action Happens and How it is Described

1) Look out for the way that the events _fit together_, and _how_ they are _caused_.
2) This is called the _plot_ — the _story_ of the text.
3) Action in a text is either _deliberate_, or happens _by chance_.
4) Take notes on _how_ the action is _described_; eg if the tone is _angry_ or _joyful_.
5) Try to work out how the language of the passage is being used to create the _tone_, the _characters_ and the _descriptions_.

"Gosh I'm cross," thought Bob.

DON'T FORGET TO ASK THE GOLDEN QUESTION:
How does the text make you react, and how has it created those reactions?

6) Why Things Turn Out The Way They Do

1) This is the _argument_ of a text — _why_ things happen the way they do.
2) Think about the whole _chain of events_ — plot, characters, setting and themes (see P.51).
3) Ask yourself what the text is _trying to say_: for example, _All Quiet on the Western Front_ by Erich Maria Remarque is about the _mindlessness of war_, and the _waste of young lives_.
4) You should also ask _why_ the text has been written in the _way_ it has — your _notes_ on _who_, _what_, _when_, _where_ and _how_ will help you to draw your own conclusions.

When you read a text, ask yourself the _six major questions_ and make a _note_ of your answers. Then you'll have a _clear understanding_ of what you have read.

Understanding texts — a questionable practice...

Remember — in a _play_ the _stage directions_ will tell you who is speaking when, and where the action is set. The problem with _reading plays_ is that they were really written to be _performed_. You must always keep this in mind when you read them. Don't forget the _six major questions_.

Context

Now that we have looked at the _six major questions_, we need to cover the idea of _context_.

Context means the Ideas around a Text

1) Context means any _additional material_ which is _relevant_ when you read a text.
2) Context material should help you to see a _larger picture_ of the text; _when_ it was written, perhaps _why_ it was written. It includes _critical books_ — what _other people_ have _said_ about the text when they read it.

REMEMBER: context material should _help_ you to explore the _ideas_ and _style_ of a text, but it _isn't_ a substitute for _reading_ the text carefully yourself.

Looking at the Author

What the Dickens shall I write about now?

Beats me guv'nor, I'm just a pen

1) Find out about the _real person_ who wrote the text; _when_ they lived, _how_ they lived and whether they were _happy_.
2) Some authors write about their own _experiences_, especially _poets_; for example the _war poets_, Wilfred Owen, Siegfried Sassoon and Rupert Brooke.
3) Some writers _imagine_ other people's experiences — Shakespeare often wrote about Kings, but was never a King in _real life_.
4) _Don't_ confuse the _author's life_ with _what happens_ in a text. Authors _change_ their real-life experiences when they write about them. _Never_ confuse _authors_ with _narrators_.
5) We don't know much about the real lives of some authors — notably _Shakespeare_ — so studying them won't help. Other writers, like _Dickens_, often drew on their own experiences.

When and Why the Text was Written

1) Check the _date_ of a text's publication — some texts are written years before being published.
2) See if the text was written _close_ to when it is _set_ — or a _long_ time _before_ or _after_: for example, George Orwell's _Nineteen Eighty-Four_ was published in _1949_.
3) Some texts are written for a _specific reason_; many _poets_ write for a particular _occasion_, like a _birth_ or a _New Year_. The _Poet Laureate_ writes poems for _State Occasions_.
4) Some authors have _patrons_ — people who _give them money_ so they can write instead of having to do another job. Authors like Shakespeare, Wordsworth and Yeats all had patrons.
5) Some authors may be _journalists_ — many of Dickens' novels appeared in _instalments_ in magazines, which means it was his job to make them _long_ and _dramatic_ to read.

Sources and Critics — Additional Information

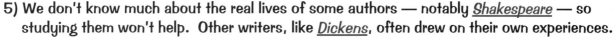

1) Many authors base their texts on _source material_; almost all of Shakespeare's plays are based on _older versions_ of the _same_ stories.
2) _Reading_ the sources shows you what an author _changed_, and perhaps _why_ it was changed.
3) _Critics_ are people who publish books _about_ texts, giving _opinions_ based on their reading. These books can be helpful to pick up _ideas_ on the _themes_ and the _style_ of a text.
4) _Don't_ just _copy_ critics though; the Examiner wants to know _your thoughts_ and _your opinions_ about a text. That means _you_ have to be able to give _reasons_ for your ideas.

Shakespeare stole his stories — imagine that...

Complicated stuff, but you must get the idea of _context_ clear in your mind. Remember — context includes any _relevant information_ which _isn't_ part of the text itself.

Context and Tone

You have a context too — where you live and who you are — and it affects _you_ when you read. Sometimes your _opinions_ about a text are _influenced_ by your _own experiences_.

Your Context Affects How You Read Texts

In the 19th century doughnuts were invented to ease constipation

1) Some texts contain things you _don't understand_, or you think are _wrong_.
2) This is because the text has a _different context_ from your own.
3) Certain texts come from _different times_ in history; others come from _different cultures_ (see Section Nine, P.98).
4) Be careful when you spot these differences — _don't_ just say that they are _wrong_, because they may be _acceptable_ in another context.
5) For example, in 19th century novels, women don't have the same _rights_ as men. When these texts were written, society _accepted_ this view. In _today's world_, women and men should be treated equally. The context has _changed_ — which changes the _meaning_.
6) Remember that all texts have an _original context_ which may be _different_ from yours — think about the context before you make up your mind about the text.
7) Find out _when_ the book was written — and what _society_ thought at the time. Some authors are very unpopular in their own time, but become popular in the context of later cultures.

A Change of Context Can Change the Meaning

In Act I, scene iii of Shakespeare's _Romeo and Juliet_, we are told that Juliet is thirteen years old. Her mother says in line 12, "She's not fourteen." In line 69 her mother says, "Well think of marriage now." She goes on to say that younger girls than Juliet are "made already mothers."

At the time when the play is set, and in Shakespeare's own time, girls were _often_ married by fourteen, usually in marriages _arranged_ by their parents. This is rare today, but helps us to understand the _original context_ of the play. Juliet is _young_ and _inexperienced_; when she falls in love with the wrong person, she is caught up in her emotions against the will of her family.

Looking for the Tone of a Text

1) Each passage in a text tries to create _different reactions_ in the reader. This affects the _atmosphere_ of the text (the main feeling).
2) The _tone_ of a piece is how it _sounds_; whether it is _angry_ or _suspicious_, _frightening_ or _funny_. Every single _sentence_ of a text has a _tone_.
3) The easiest way to _judge_ the tone of a passage is to read it _out loud_. Think about how the words should _sound_, and the _emotion_ they express.
4) _Practise_ reading short passages from _different books_ in different _styles_. After a while you should try to _sound out_ the sentences when you read the passage _in your head_. I know this sounds ridiculous but it _actually works_ if you practise long enough.
5) It'll help you to _judge the tone_ of any passage you read. This is especially useful in _Exams_ where you have to do _comprehension exercises_ on passages you've never seen before.

BE CAREFUL: tone is not the same as style. _Style_ means the particular forms of language and structure used. _Tone_ means the feel of the piece; the effect a passage has on the reader. Don't confuse the two in your essays.

Feeling the music of language — a matter of tone...

Context is a complex business, I'm afraid, but you do need to understand how it _affects_ your reading. Don't forget the _difference_ between _style_ and _tone_ — try to practise reading for tone.

Imagery

Now we're going to look at _how_ authors create _effects_ with language — starting with imagery.

All Texts Use Images to Create Pictures

1) Images are _descriptions_ that create a picture of the thing they describe. They help to bring a text _to life_, and create a sense of _tone_: eg "My love is like a _red, red rose_" (from Robert Burns).

2) An image can be used _once_, or it can be _continued_ through a passage, and _expanded_ in different ways:

3) Let's take an example from _Romeo and Juliet_, Act I, scene v. This is the first scene where Romeo and Juliet _meet_ and speak to each other. Both of them are _attracted_ to the other, and the scene shows them _flirting_:

> **Romeo:** If I profane with my unworthiest hand,
> This holy shrine, the gentle sin is this,
> My lips, two blushing pilgrims, ready stand
> To smooth that rough touch with a tender kiss.
> **Juliet:** Good pilgrim, you do wrong your hand too much,
> Which mannerly devotion shows in this:
> For saints have hands that pilgrims' hands do touch
> And palm to palm is holy palmers' kiss.

TALKING ABOUT THE IMAGES

1) The image of Juliet as a "_shrine_" is used throughout this passage.

2) Romeo says his lips are "_pilgrims_" to the shrine — offering to kiss her.

3) Juliet says that _pilgrim's hand_ often touch _saint's hands_; so they should go "_palm to palm_" — and _hold hands_ in a holy kiss.

4) The whole passage is an image of the _instant attraction_ between the two. Juliet answers Romeo by repeating the _same style_ of poetry he speaks, using the _same rhymes_ of "this" and "kiss," and using the _same images_ of pilgrims, shrines and sin.

Good night, good night! Parting is such sweet sorrow, That I shall say good night till it be morrow.

The Two Key Forms of Image — Similes and Metaphors

1) _Similes_ compare two things — showing there is a point of _similarity_ between them. Similes must always use one of the _similarity words_: like, as, as if, as though, as...as.

eg My love is like a red, red rose That's newly sprung in June: My love is like a melody That's sweetly played in tune. ("A Red, Red Rose", Robert Burns)	The poet's love is likened to a newly grown red rose and a sweet, tuneful melody. The poem tries to give images of what it is like to be in love, and how beautiful and natural the feeling is.

2) _Metaphors_ are _images_ where one thing is said _to be_ something else. These images aren't literally true, but they create an _impression_ of what something is like. They are much more _vivid_ and _immediate_ than similes: eg Some critics say that Shakespeare was a magpie.

This _doesn't_ mean that Shakespeare was really a black and white bird; it means that he used to _steal ideas_ from anywhere he could find them, in the same way that a real _magpie_ will _steal_ all sorts of _objects_ that it finds.

Who's a pretty bard then?

> **REMEMBER:** similes are _like_ something; metaphors actually _are_ that thing.

As friendly as a llama — a spitting image

Remember the difference between _similes_ and _metaphors_. They are incredibly useful definitions to use when you write about _imagery_ in texts. Practise _recognising_ them in different kinds of text.

Poetic Language

Even _newspapers_ use poetic language to make sentences and headlines sound _memorable_. It's about using language to make _word music_, and packing in _everything_ you want to say as well.

The Four Main Elements of Poetic Language

1) Rhyme

1) Rhyme means that two words _sound the same_ — even if they're spelt differently. It's what most people recognise in poetry.
2) Rhymes can come at the _end_ of two lines, or in the _middle_ of a line. Be careful though; many poems _don't_ use rhyme, particularly modern pieces.

> Out flew the web and floated _wide_;
> The mirror crack'd from _side_ to _side_;
> 'The curse is come upon me,' _cried_
> The Lady of Shallott.
> ("_The Lady of Shallott,_"
> Part III; Lord Tennyson)

2) Assonance

1) Assonance means two words _sound similar_, because they share a _vowel_ sound. Unlike rhyme, the consonant sound _doesn't_ have to be the same.
2) The _spelling_ of the words _doesn't_ matter: only the _sound_ is important: eg _week_, _peace_ and _weep_.

> Then a mile of warm _sea_-scented _beach_;
> _Three_ _fields_ to cross till a farm _appears_;
> A _tap_ _at_ the pain, the quick _sharp_ _scratch_
> And _blue_ _spurt_ of a lighted _match_,
> ("_Meeting at Night,_"
> Robert Browning)

3) Alliteration

1) Alliteration means that a _series_ of words _repeat_ the same _consonant_. It's very common in poetry and sometimes in prose texts:

> Where though_ts_ _s_erenely _s_weet expre_ss_
> How pure, how dear their dwelling-place.
> ("_She walks in beauty,_" Lord Byron)

2) In Anglo-Saxon times, _all_ English poetry used alliteration _instead_ of rhyme, like the epic poem _Beowulf_.
3) In the 14th Century, several popular poems revived alliteration: eg _The Vision of Piers Plowman_.
4) Nowadays, alliteration is common in _tabloid headlines_: eg Rock Star in Road Rage Rant Shock.

> **WARNING: don't talk about alliteration if there are only two words in the text which share the same letter — these are not clear enough examples.**

4) Half-Rhyme

1) Half-rhyme is where words share _similar consonants_ but have _different vowel sounds_.
2) It's sometimes used in poetry as a _variation_ from standard rhyme.
3) It can create a _mysterious_ tone: eg Wilfred Owen's "Strange Meeting," or the Fool's prophecy in Shakespeare's play _King Lear_.

> **Fool:** When usurers tell their gold i'the'_field_,
> And bawds and whores do churches _build_;
> (_King Lear_, Act III, scene ii;
> William Shakespeare)

Poetic language — rhyme and reasons...

Phew! All these types of _word music_ are used to create effects. When you read a text, you need to look for these features and say what _effect_ they create; if they give a clearer _image_, or a certain _tone_, perhaps. Remember; the easiest way to find these features is to read the text out loud. Learn how all these poetic features _sound_ — practise by reading the extracts on this page.

More Literary Language

Here are some more types of *literary language* — make sure you *learn* how to *identify* each one.

Onomatopoeia *is when a word* sounds like *what it* means

1) This a form of *word music* that writers love to use, especially
   when they describe *noises*:
   eg   words like bang, crash, pop, whisper, and hush.
2) Onomatopoeia is also used to give an idea of *movement*:
   eg The vampire *creeps* slowly towards her sleeping victim.
       The snake *hissed* and *slithered* away.
3) It gives the reader a *clearer image*.

Exaggeration *is used to* Emphasise a Point

1) Exaggeration is often used in *imagery*, to make something seem especially *important*:
   eg "Come not between the dragon and his wrath;" (*King Lear*, Act I, scene i)
       Lear compares himself to a dragon, exaggerating the power of his anger against Cordelia.
2) Exaggeration is also used for *comic effect*, to make something seem *ridiculous*.

Jonathan Swift uses *comic exaggeration* in an essay called "A Modest Proposal" (1729), where he suggests that rich people should *eat* the children of the poor, since they are treated so badly anyway. He says that this would be "innocent, cheap, easy and effectual." Obviously he didn't mean this literally; he is *exaggerating* to make a point about how the rich treat the poor in Ireland using a vivid image.

Personification — *describing* Things as People

1) This is common in *poetry*, where ideas and objects are described with *human characteristics*.

   For example, John Keats' poem
   "To Autumn," describes Autumn
   as a human being:

   > Sometimes whoever seeks abroad may find
   > Thee sitting careless on a granary floor,
   > Thy hair soft-lifted by the winnowing wind,

2) Making an *idea* or an *object* seem human gives it a *clearer image*.
   It helps the reader to *identify* with something more closely. This is
   why *sailors* call their *ships*, "she," as though the ship was a woman.
3) It's also why we talk about *Jack Frost*, or *Death* (a skeleton with a
   scythe), *Father Time* and *Mother Nature*. These have their origins in
   superstitions.

Synonyms — *Using a* Wide Vocabulary

1) Synonyms are *different words* that mean the *same thing*. Authors use synonyms to *avoid repeating* the same language, which would make their texts boring to read.
2) The best way to *learn* synonyms is by increasing your vocabulary; *learning new words*.
   Make sure you *look up* new words you find when you're reading. Use a *dictionary*.
3) There is also a special dictionary of synonyms, called a *thesaurus*. When you look up a
   word, all the different synonyms are listed. See if you can find one in your local library.

Be like Coleridge — *he knew what a word's worth...*

Make sure you *learn* these literary tricks carefully. Examiners will give *high marks* if you can
identify these features in a text and *write about them* in your essays. The secret is giving an
example — it *proves* that you know what you're doing and that you really *deserve* the marks.

Looking at Old Texts

Whether you're studying _English_ or _English Literature_, you'll have to read and study _old texts_ as well as _modern_ ones.

Watch out for Language and Spelling

1) The language and spelling in old texts can be very _different_ from _modern_ Standard English.
2) Most texts from the _19th_ and _20th Centuries_ are printed in modern English. Some words may have _slightly different meanings_.
3) In _19th Century_ texts, _sentences_ tend to be much _longer_ than in texts written in the last 50 years. You'll get used to that.
4) In texts written _before_ the 19th Century, many words have _changed meaning_ over time. Read the text _around_ the word to _check_ what it means — _never_ assume it means exactly the same thing.

Do you speak English sir?

Ugg?

Finding out the _old meaning_ of the word can help you to discover what a text's _imagery_ really means.

Bassanio: What find I here?
          [_opening the leaden casket_]
Fair Portia's _counterfeit_! What demigod
Hath come so near creation?
(_The Merchant of Venice_, Act III, scene ii;
          William Shakespeare)

Counterfeit doesn't mean a forgery here; it means a _portrait_. In Shakespeare's time, the word meant the portrait of a King which appeared on a coin; Bassanio is using it as an image of _Portia's portrait_ inside the casket, and also an image of the _wealth_ he has won by choosing the right casket and winning Portia's hand in marriage. Over time the word came to mean a fake coin made to look like a real one.

Old Forms of Language are sometimes Used

1) Some words are just _old-fashioned_. In many old texts, _thee_ and _thou_ are used to mean _you_ in the _singular_; _ye_ is a form of you in the _plural_. _Thy_ means _your_.
2) Other common old-fashioned forms include: _doth_ meaning _does_; _hath_ meaning _has_; _art_ meaning _are_. Many verb forms end in the letters _-st_: eg wouldst, willst, goest etc.
3) _Don't_ be put off by these forms. They look more complicated than they really are.

REMEMBER: in poetry, the usual word order of English can be changed to make the line sound better; this often means that the verb changes position.

eg   "Not from the stars do I my judgement pluck," (Sonnet XIV, William Shakespeare)
      = I don't pluck my judgement (draw conclusions) from the stars.

Beware of Spelling in Old Texts

1) Until the _18th Century_, spellings in English _weren't_ fixed. People spelt things as they _wanted_.
2) Even _Shakespeare_ couldn't spell — he used to write his _own name_ using several _different_ spellings. That _doesn't_ mean you can forget _your spelling_ though — you will _lose marks_.
3) When you _quote_ from texts with bad spelling, _leave_ the spelling _as it is_ in the original, but make sure you use _quotation marks_ (see P.29).

NOTE: don't be put off old texts because the language is different. There are a lot of stories worth reading. You can always find good, clear versions of old texts in modern English to help you.

I blame Chaucer — he was always telling tales...

Old texts sound dull, I know, but you'd be surprised how funny some of _The Canterbury Tales_ are. Don't forget — you can always start with a _modern version_, but you will need to look at the _original text_ as part of your course. Just read it _carefully_; remember that meanings can _change_.

Commenting on your Reading

You must be able to _give an opinion_ about what you have read, based on the _key features_ of _style_ and _tone_ which you have recognised.

Forming an Opinion about a Text

1) Read the text first. The _history_ of a text, the life of its _author_ and the _context_ in which it was written are useless unless you _read_ the text.
2) You must be ready to _quote_ from the text. You'll need to give _examples_ from the text to _back up_ your opinion of it. Look at the Section on Writing Skills to help you here.
3) Don't worry if your opinion isn't the same as _other people's_ — just make certain you can _back it up_ with lots of _examples_ from the text.
4) _Look up_ the meanings of words you don't know, and be especially careful with _old_ texts.
5) Practise _recognising_ the key features of _style_ and _tone_ — you will definitely need to learn the main elements of _poetic language_.
6) Read other texts too — Examiners will give _high marks_ to students who show that they have read _other texts_ that are _relevant_ to a text they're studying. Just make sure the text is _relevant:_
   eg   If you're studying the War Poets, read _All Quiet on the Western Front_, by Erich Maria Remarque, and _Goodbye to all That_, by Robert Graves.
7) If you're asked a _specific question_ about a text, you must _only_ answer that question. _Don't_ include irrelevant details just because you've learned them — you'll _lose marks_.

The Themes of a Text are What it is About

1) In this Section we've concentrated on the _context_, the _style_ and the _tone_ of a text.
2) You will also have to know about the _themes_ — what the text is about.
3) This _doesn't just_ mean the _story_, _characters_, _imagery_ and _language_. It means the _main ideas_ behind the text. You can only find these out by _reading_ the text _closely_ — by asking the _six major questions_, by taking _accurate notes_ and by finding the _important quotations_.
4) From these you should be able to work out the _main themes_. Any _context_ information will help you, as will any _introduction_ to the text: eg One of the key themes of _Macbeth_ is the divine nature of Kingship — how the natural order of the universe is upset when Macbeth seizes power.
5) Most texts have _more than one_ theme — particularly _novels_ and _plays_. It may help you to organise your _notes_ for a text into its _key themes:_

   eg _Great Expectations_ = Snobbery, Love, Friendship, Portable Property, Revenge.

Making a Drama out of a Play text

1) Play texts are a _special case_ — they were written to be _performed_. _Don't_ decide you understand a play before you _see it_ performed.
2) _Remember:_ any performance of a play is just one _interpretation_ — particularly when you watch a _Shakespeare_ play. _Critics_ and _theatre directors_ interpret Shakespeare in many _different_ ways.

One last thing — read all about it...

Enjoy your reading: there's _no point_ in worrying about Exams the first time you read a text. Otherwise you'll end up hating it. Texts were written to be _read_, not studied. So start by just reading the book, as if you were _scanning_. It may be hard, it may take some time, but at least you _won't_ hate it; and that means you'll _write_ about it _much better_. Try it and see.

Revision Summary for Section Five

This is a very important Section to understand, because without it you won't be able to make any sense of Section Seven on Essay Writing Skills. Take some time now to go over the Section again, making sure that you've understood everything. When you feel confident and ready, then have a go at these revision questions. Remember — this exercise is about finding out what you know and what you still need to learn. Don't cheat by looking back over the Section — there's no point. That won't help you in the Exam. Have a go at the questions first, then go back and look over any areas you weren't sure about.

1) What are the three key features of style? *the language used the Vocabulary used the Tone*
2) What are the six major questions? *who, what, where, when, how, why*
3) Which four of these are fairly straightforward? *who where when what*
4) Which are the tricky two? *how why*
5) What's the difference between authors and narrators? *所作者*
6) How are narrators biased when they tell a story?
7) Explain why things don't just happen by accident in literary texts?
8) Why do you need to know when the events in a text take place?
9) Why do you need to know when the narrator is speaking?
10) What is the Golden Question?
11) Why is it important to find out why things happen the way they do?
12) What is context?
13) Why should you think about an author's sources?
14) How does your context affect how you read texts?
15) What should you never say about cultural and historical contexts?
16) What's the difference between style and tone?
17) What are the two key forms of imagery?
18) Name the four main elements of poetic language.
19) What is assonance, and how does it differ from rhyme?
20) Where is alliteration most common? Give an example of a sentence using alliteration.
21) What is half-rhyme, and what tone does it create?
22) What term describes a word that sounds like what it means?
23) Why do writers sometimes talk about things as if they were people? What do we call this?
24) What is the correct term for words that mean the same thing?
25) What should you look out for in texts written before the 19th century?
26) If you're not sure whether a word means what you think it does, what should you do?
27) What are the modern forms of: doth; goest; art; thy?
28) When was English spelling fixed?
29) What are the themes of a text?
30) How do you find out the themes of a text?
31) Write a short essay about a book you read recently, using the skills in this Section. Start by asking the six major questions, then write about the style and the tone of the book. If you know anything about the context of the book then write about that too.
32) Find a short poem and read it carefully. Make a note of any features of poetic language it contains. What is the theme of the poem?

Non-Fiction and Media Texts

For your English course, you'll have to read _non-fiction_ texts as well as fiction. _Don't panic_ though — the skills you need are exactly the same.

Everything We Read _or Watch_ _is Biased_

I don't need the internet to find out about people

1) During the 20th Century, the amount of _information_ being stored and produced has increased massively.

2) This doesn't just mean _books_ and _plays;_ it includes _newspapers_, _films_, _television_ and _radio programmes_, _adverts_ and the _internet_.

3) These _sources_ of information are called the _media:_ they present us with different _views_ of the world, for _entertainment_ or for _news_.

4) All media are _biased:_ they present an _opinion_ of the truth rather than the _whole_ truth. This is because they are _affected_ by their _context_ (see PP.45-46) and their _culture_ (see P.97).

5) Even _news_ programmes are biased: _American_ television news focuses on _different_ stories from _British_ programmes. This is because some stories are more _relevant_ in the USA than in Britain.

6) Any _information_ is a _text_ that can be looked at _critically_. That means reading it _carefully_, using your _comprehension skills_ (see Section Four, P.35); looking at the _context_, and trying to work out what the text is _saying_, and what _opinion_ it is putting forward.

> BEWARE: many media texts claim to be unbiased and say that they present only the truth. Don't believe them. Make sure you look at them critically.

What to Look For _in Non-Fiction_ Texts

1) Just because something is _non-fiction_, this doesn't mean it isn't _biased_. In fact, many of the _tricks_ non-fiction writers use are the _same_ as the ones used in _fiction_ (see Section Five, P.42).

2) Look at the _style_ of the text. You need to look at the _language_, _tone_ and _vocabulary_ used, and the _context_. When you read the text, ask yourself the _six major questions_ (PP.43-4).

The Top Five Tricks _used in Non-Fiction Texts_

1) Check any _information_ given, especially _statistics_, to see if anything important has been _left out_. Many texts _generalise_; they say something is true in _all_ cases when there are _exceptions_.

2) See if _emotional vocabulary_ has been used — _language_ gives clear _clues_ to the bias of the text: eg some news reports may say _"limited air strikes"_; others, _"illegal military interference."_

3) Information can be _exaggerated_ to make it sound more _interesting:_ eg _"Music Star Marriage on the Rocks"_ sounds more exciting than _"Married Music Stars have a Tiff."_

4) Watch out for _tone:_ whether the presentation is _serious_ or _comic:_   eg   some interviewers describe the bad habits of the person they interview if they want to present a negative opinion.

5) _Opinions_ are often presented as though they were _facts_. This is difficult to detect, but it affects whether or not we _believe_ and _trust_ that text. Many news reports _speculate_ about what will happen in the future — these are not facts but _opinions_.

Television _and Film_ _are Texts Too_

1) It might seem a little strange to talk about film and TV as _texts_, but they _are_.

2) Even though people appear to be _talking_ to you in film and TV, they are usually speaking from a _written script_. The _language_ used is a _written_ text made to sound like _natural speech_.

3) That's why it is very _important_ to study media _language_, especially on _television_ — because it's often trying to sound as _natural_ as possible. It can tell you a lot about how real people speak.

4) TV and film include other elements _apart from_ language: _visual pictures_, _music_, _sound effects_, _architecture_ (sets) and _lighting_. You need to practise _recognising_ how these elements help create _effects_ that provoke responses in viewers — in similar ways to the _theatre_.

Fiction vs Fact

When you look at _any_ text, you must _first_ decide whether it is a piece of _fiction_ or not. Unfortunately, the distinction _isn't_ always that _clear_.

Non-Fiction texts aren't always Factual

This proves our wigs are 100% more realistic

Dodgy Tests

1) Once you have learned to recognise the _styles_ of different kinds of _non-fiction_ text, you should be able to identify any _bias_ in the text, and any _confusion_ between _facts_ and _opinion_.

2) _Many_ non-fiction texts are _deliberately_ written as a _mixture_ of fact and opinion. A good _essay_ contains both fact _and_ opinion. _Newspaper editorials_ do the same.

3) If a text puts forward an _argument_, then it will give opinions _based on_ the facts, and will use facts as _examples_ to illustrate their points. Sometimes the text will _say clearly_ when it is giving an opinion, sometimes it _won't_. You will need to _read carefully_ for opinions and facts.

4) Many texts use _quotations_ from other texts. This is one way to _back up_ an argument, but the _source_ of the quotation _must_ be given. Look for the _place_, the _author/speaker_ and the _date_.

5) Some texts will use _quotations_ as though they _are_ facts. Be very _careful_; many quotations just give _someone else's opinion_: eg quotations from essays on Shakespeare by literary critics; the opinion of the Prime Minister's Press Officer on the success of the government.

6) Many _news reports_ today are a _mixture_ of fact and opinion. Reporters tell the story of some _people involved_ in a news event — we hear _what happened_ and their _opinion_ of the event. The report has been _written_ to make you respond _emotionally_, or to make you _laugh_ — it doesn't just contain factual information.

Always look out for the relationship between facts and opinions in any non-fiction text you read. It will give you lots to write about in Coursework or Exam essays.

Some Fiction is written in the Style of Non-Fiction

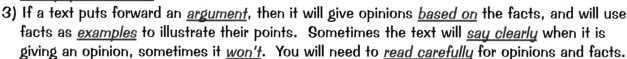

Yes Cathy, I'm not your husband Ryan... I'm his evil half brother Danforth!

No, I can't believe it... But I love you anyway.

1) Many authors use the _language_ and _tone_ of non-fiction texts when they write — some novels use _letters_ or _diaries_ to tell the story: eg _Bridget Jones' Diary_ by Helen Fielding.

2) Sometimes authors include _reports_ from fictional _newspapers_, or _police_ reports, to make their stories sound _authentic_.

3) Many _soap operas_ on TV and radio are written in the _style_ of _documentaries_. The writers try to make the _characters_ and _situations_ seem _real_, even though they aren't. Of course, some soap operas aren't very _realistic_ at all.

4) This sort of _real-life_ presentation is most commonly seen in _adverts_: when a company wants you to _buy_ a product, they want to _amuse_ you and make you feel that you _need_ that product.

5) When you read a text, look for _signs_ that it might be written in a _non-fiction style_, and ask yourself what _effect_ the author is trying to create. Over the next few pages, we'll look at the _styles_ and _tones_ of some popular non-fiction texts that will come up in your _Course_ or _Exam_.

Fiction and Fact — forming a faction...

There's plenty to watch out for when you're looking at _non-fiction texts_, especially media texts. You must always read closely for _fact_ and _opinion_ — it'll help you to work out the _bias_ of the text. Remember the _top five tricks_; find two examples of each in any newspaper and learn them.

The Media

The word media is literally *"the means"* by which something is done. Nowadays it's used to mean the *news* media — *television*, *radio* and *newspapers* etc.

Newspapers *have Several Different Styles*

1) *Every* newspaper has a *basic style* — either it's a *tabloid* or a *broadsheet*. Tabloids are *easier* to *read* and tend to focus on *sensational* stories with big, bold headlines.

2) Tabloids often *mix* fact with opinion in the *same* article — they often use *biased* and *emotional* language.

3) Some tabloids operate *rules* about how *many* stories can appear on each page, and *restrict* the *number* of news stories so that they can include stories about famous *stars* or *scandals*.

4) Broadsheets are *large* newspapers that fold in half. They tend to be more *serious* in tone, and are *separated* into different *sections* which contain different styles of article.

5) Most *opinion* articles are clearly *marked*, so that the reader can tell they are opinion not fact.

6) *Reporting* tends to be divided up into *news* reporting, *analysis* and *opinion* (editorial section), *lifestyle* articles (health, travel and food, for example), *interviews*, *reviews* of books, films or cultural events, *sports* reports and sometimes *extracts* from new books.

Read all about it

Reading *Newspapers to find their Style*

Here is a sample extract. Read it carefully and *learn* how to spot the *key features* of its *style*.

Chukka Your Man Celine!
Celeb Chef's Life of Hell with Love Rat Hewley
by Our Special Correspondent

Celebrity chef Celine Strimpet broke down in tears yesterday as she spoke about her unhappy marriage to polo legend James Hewley. Hewley, 37, was sensationally photographed **cheating** at polo and **enjoying** the

attentions of a dusky Argentine beauty at a toff's polo match in Buenos Aires last week.

Key Features

1) The headline has a *pun* (play on words) to draw the reader in. The sub heading gives the *outline* of the story.

2) The piece uses *emotional language*: Hewley is described unsympathetically as a "love rat" at a "toff's polo match."

3) The piece is *biased* — it begins with Celine bursting into tears, and *highlights* two negative words about Hewley's behaviour, cheating and enjoying.

4) Hewley's *age* and his *cheating* at polo are *irrelevant* if the article is just about his marriage.

5) By adding *extra* facts, the article gives an opinion which *appears* to be based on lots of *evidence*. It *doesn't* actually give any *specific evidence*; even about the girl in Argentina.

6) The story is about two *famous* people, and it is presented in a *sensational*, *exaggerated* tone.

7) Everything about the piece is written to demand a *response* from the reader — "her unhappy marriage" suggests that the marriage was *only* unhappy *for her*.

8) The phrase "sensationally photographed" *suggests* that the pictures give *clear evidence* of Hewley's cheating — but the photos are not printed, so *no evidence* is offered at all.

The 'papers are biased — it's all news to me...

Reading newspapers is a great way to practise your *critical skills*. You could be given a newspaper article in your *Exam*, or as part of your *coursework* — see if you can remember the *top five tricks*. Look for the key features of *style* as well as the content of the piece.

Newspapers and Magazines

Features are the most common kind of article you'll come across in _Exams_ or _Coursework_. These are _longer_ than news stories and usually look _in depth_ at a particular story. That means they present an _argument_, with _facts_ and a variety of _opinions_, often taken from short _interviews_.

The Difference between Magazines and Newspapers

1) Magazines and newspapers are _written_ for different _reasons_.
2) A _magazine_ focuses on _features_ and news centred on a _particular subject_ or written for a _particular group_ of people: for example, football or music magazines, women's or men's magazines, car enthusiasts' magazines etc.

> I wonder if Velcro Monthly's out yet...

3) _Newspapers_ are _daily_ or _weekly_ publications; _magazines_ are usually _monthly_.
4) Because magazines are written with a _specific audience_ in mind, the articles are often written in a particular _style_ or _tone_ — whenever you read a magazine extract, make sure you know _where_ it came from. Think about how the _context_ is going to _affect_ the text — look for the _five tricks_.

Recognising the Style of a Feature Article

This sample extract shows the style of a _feature article_.

Where the Sun Never Shines

by Marina Sankey in London; additional reporting Zelba Rievers.

For thousands of years mankind has looked to the heavens for inspiration. In Ancient Greece, astronomers searched the stars, believing them to be forms of the almighty Gods. During the Renaissance, Galileo looked for the order of the universe through his telescope. Now one scientist believes he has at last uncovered one of the mysteries of the stars — their origin.

"People talk about the Big Bang theory as though it has been scientifically proved. It hasn't!" Jed Weiner hits the table with a baseball bat as he says this; so I am inclined to accept whatever he chooses to say.

We are sitting in Weiner's Honolulu Office, from which he runs his freelance astronomy agency. "Ever since NASA kicked me out, they've been trying to destroy my funding and discredit my research. Well

not any more! No way, my friend!"

Weiner's puffy red face is inches from my own. This is one of the most brilliant astronomers of his age; I don't want to offend him by laughing. cont.

1) The _theme_ of the article is _less obvious_ than in a news report. The _headline_ only makes sense when you start to read the article.
2) The _subject_ of the article isn't introduced until the _end_ of the first paragraph. The _tone_ of the article is more _leisurely_ and _well-researched_, but it is also _smug_ and _mocking_.
3) It gives details about _Greece_ and _Galileo_ in order to sound _knowledgeable_ about astronomy.
4) The _interview_ with Jed Weiner is described in a _comic_ tone of voice. The writer _mocks_ Weiner by telling us he has a _baseball bat_, and she's trying not to _laugh_ at him. He is _made_ to seem _odd_.

Beauty magazines — they must have good features...

Feature articles are common in _Reading Exams_ — you must _learn_ how to spot the style and tone. Remember — newspapers and magazines are written in _columns_, so read them that way.

Adverts

Adverts try to _manipulate_ our feelings in order to _make us_ buy a product. You may have to _compare_ a series of adverts in a comprehension exercise, or write about the _effects_ of advertising.

Adverts are about Selling Products

1) Sounds simple enough, but some adverts _hide_ their product behind a _story_ or a _celebrity_. We don't realise they're just _selling_ something.
2) You need to _learn_ to look at them _critically_.
3) Adverts often use the _top five tricks_. Be particularly careful with any _statistics_ they give — most are _confusing_ (see below).
4) Adverts appear in many forms: _posters_, pages in _magazines_, _television_ adverts etc.

Did you know 98.4% of all statistics are misleading - including this one?

> **REMEMBER:** even though adverts come in different forms, they use the same tricks of tone, language and context to try to sell their products.

Statistics can be Manipulated

1) Many adverts use statistics to _prove a point_. They claim that statistics are _facts_ and cannot be wrong. Presenting statistics this way makes them _seem_ like _scientific truth_.
2) Statistics can be _misleading_ though, especially if they aren't very _specific_.

WHITE ON
Washing Powder
THE RIGHT CHOICE FOR BRIGHT WHITE

Example: "White On: Nine out of ten customers prefer it."

This statistic looks impressive, but you must ask if it's specific enough.
a) It doesn't say _who_ the customers are. If we don't know who they are, we _can't tell_ if the statistic is impressive or not. The survey might only have asked ten customers _altogether_.
b) It doesn't say _what_ they prefer White On to — there's _no real comparison_ between White On and its rivals. Perhaps they prefer White On to dirty clothes, which isn't much of a recommendation.

> The advert gives an impressive-sounding statistic which doesn't actually mean much at all. Look out for statistics like this, which give no real evidence.

3) _Remember_ — many non-fiction texts use statistics to _support their arguments_, from newspaper articles to history books. Ask yourself whether the statistics give any _real_ evidence.

Some Adverts use Experts to make you believe them

1) Adverts may use a _scientist_ or a _top breeder_ to recommend a product. We accept what _they_ say because we are told they are _experts_.
2) The fact that they are experts is _irrelevant_. They have been _paid_ to say how good a product is.
3) _Scientific tests_ may _claim_ to prove a product is better than "our leading competitor" — but won't say _who_ the competitor is. _Watch out_ for so-called experts.

Adverts Use Slogans to Stick in Your Head

1) Slogans are _easy-to-remember_ phrases which stay in your head and _remind_ you of the product in an advert.
2) They often use the tricks of _poetic language_ (see P.48).
3) They also appeal to our _fantasies_ — the kind of _lifestyle_ we want to have — and to our _worries_ — such as whether we're _overweight_ or _unpopular_.
4) Advertising can _influence_ people in _negative_ ways — it reinforces _stereotypes_ about thin people being beautiful, for example. This is a popular _Exam essay_ topic.

TAHITI - BECAUSE SHE'S WORTH IT

Film and TV

Part of your _Coursework_ may include writing a _review_ or an _essay_ on a _film_ or _TV programme_ you've watched. To pick up _good marks_, you'll need to use your _critical skills_ to interpret them.

Film and TV are not the same

1) Film and TV are _similar_ media, because they use the same tricks of _sound_, _pictures_, _light_ and _music_.
2) _Television_ pictures are formed by tiny _dots_ of light — _film_ pictures are formed by shining a light through a roll of _tape_.
3) Films are shown in _cinemas_ and people _pay_ to see them.
4) TV is shown on _television sets_, and shows all kinds of programmes. It's paid for by _sponsorship_ — either by _advertising_ or by a _licence fee_, like the BBC.
5) _Don't forget_ the difference — _film makers_ spend much more _money_ making and advertising their product because they need _as many people as possible_ to see it. Most films tell a _complete story_, so that people feel it was _worth seeing_.
6) Television companies want to have the biggest _share_ of viewers, so they try to produce a _variety_ of programmes that will keep people watching. TV programmes often tell _part_ of a story, so that you will watch the _next_ episode to see what happens — like _soap operas_.

Films and TV programmes can be fiction or non-fiction — both use the same techniques to affect you. The secret of TV and film is how they make you feel.

What to Look for in Films

I said cut!

1) Look at what _kind_ of film it is — _fiction_ or _documentary_ (non-fiction film).
2) Look at _where_ it was made — this will tell you the _context_.
3) Think about which _characters_ are _sympathetic_ and which ones seem _evil_. Decide how the story made you _feel_.
4) Think about how the film _looks_ — _bright_ or _dark_, _colourful_ or not.
5) Listen to the _music_ at the beginning and _during_ the film — think how it makes you _feel_.
6) Ask yourself if the film was _realistic_ or not — whether the story and characters were _believable_.
7) Think about whether the film _kept_ your _attention_ — if the events happened very _fast_, or if the action was _slow-moving_; if there was a serious _point_, or the film was just _fun_.
8) Decide whether you think it was a _good_ or _bad_ film — but make sure you can give your _reasons_. _Remember_ — this is your _opinion_; other people may see it differently.

Watching Television — without being a couch potato

1) Television programmes come in many forms — _documentaries_, _game shows_, _chat shows_ etc.
2) Each form of programme has its own _style_ — soap operas are _realistic_ or _fantasy_, chat shows are usually _funny_ and news programmes are almost always _serious_.
3) Think about the way _pictures_ and _music_ are used to create a _tone_ — especially in _documentaries_. _Remember_ — most documentaries _mix_ fact and opinion.
4) Listen to the way people on TV _talk_ — they may seem like they're talking _to you_, but they're usually reading a _script_. On news programmes they will sound _serious_ and use _formal_ language; on chat shows people will sound _friendly_ and _jokey_. Listen out for the _language_ and _tone_.

See your name in lights — become an electrician...

Remember — the music, pictures and words of a film or television programme have been _chosen_ to _make_ you feel what the director wants you to feel. To pick up _top marks_ in essay work, you need to show _how_ these tricks are being used. That means watching and listening _carefully_.

SECTION SIX — READING NON-FICTION

Autobiographies, Diaries, Biographies

Time to look at the main types of non-fiction _book_. They're often _easier_ to read than fiction, which means you can pick up _lots of marks_ for writing about them.

Autobiographies give a Personal View of Events

 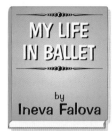

1) Most autobiographies are written by _famous people_.
2) They give a _personal_ view of the events of their lives, and often include stories about their _careers_, the people they _worked with_ and their _private_ lives.
3) People read autobiographies because they _enjoy_ finding out about the lives of the _famous_ — the same reason why people read _tabloids_.
4) Most autobiographies are _light-hearted_, but some authors use them to make _serious points_. Recently there have been books about living with _cancer_, by _John Diamond_ and _Ruth Picardie_.
5) _Fiction_ writers often write in the _style_ of an autobiography. This is called a _first person_ narrative, because the story is told using _"I"_ and _"me"_.
6) Autobiographies give _information_ on how things have _changed_ during a person's life — they are often written by _artists_, _actors_, _politicians_ and _journalists_.

REMEMBER: autobiographies are _biased_. Writers _change_ the events of their lives to make themselves _look good_, and to _simplify_ the past. Some _blame_ other people for their mistakes, or _admit_ them, claiming they have _reformed_.

Diaries are Personal Daily Records

Dear diary, today didn't go entirely to plan...

1) A _diary_ or a _journal_ is a record of what one person thinks, feels and experiences _day by day_. Don't forget — it's an _opinion_.
2) Diaries are _private_ books — usually only written for the _author_ to read. People don't keep many _secrets_ from themselves, so they often _admit_ things in diaries that they wouldn't admit in _letters_ or _formal_ writing. They are very _direct_ in style.
3) Some diaries are _published_ after the writer's _death_ — particularly diaries written by _famous_ people or by _writers_.
4) Some are _published_ because they are very _entertaining_, and because they give lots of information about _daily life_ at the time they were written — _Samuel Pepys_ kept a detailed diary of daily life between 1660 and 1669, which is a valuable _historical source_.
5) The best diaries give a sense of what it _felt_ like to be alive at a certain time — _The Diary of Anne Frank_ records the life of a young Jewish girl living during the Second World War. She tells us about life hiding from the Nazis. She died in a Concentration Camp.

Biographies are Life Stories Written by Other People

1) Biographies tell the _life stories_ of famous people — but they are written by _someone else_.
2) They can be _accurate_, _researched_ books, or they can be full of _scandal_ and _gossip_. One of the best written biographies in English is James Boswell's _Life of Dr Johnson_.
3) Make sure you look for clear _evidence_ to support any argument in a biography.
4) All biographies are _biased_ — many writers will include a _controversial_ fact or opinion in a biography so that they start an _argument_ in the _media_. This is a way to get free _publicity_.

Life stories — better than the alternative...

These types of book can win you easy marks — and you can read books _you enjoy_. That makes them perfect for _Coursework essays_. Just remember to watch out for _bias_ and _evidence_.

Letters, Travel and Criticism

Three more popular non-fiction styles here — make sure you _know_ about each one. Examiners always give good marks for _Coursework essays_ on _different types_ of non-fiction texts — it makes a change from newspaper articles all the time.

Looking at People's Collected Letters

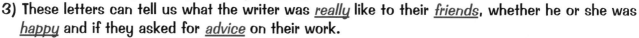

Dear Bob,
City lost at home this week...
Problems with the Sphinx...
How are your onions?...

1) Some people write letters to their _friends_ or for _business_ reasons over a period of many _years_.

2) Often these correspondences are _published_ after the writer's _death_, if the person was _famous_ — in books of Collected Letters: for example, the poet _Philip Larkin's_ letters.

3) These letters can tell us what the writer was _really_ like to their _friends_, whether he or she was _happy_ and if they asked for _advice_ on their work.

4) Sometimes an _author's_ letters to a _publisher_ or an _editor_ can show whether a book had to be _rewritten_ much before it was printed. _T.S. Eliot's_ famous poem _The Waste Land_ was heavily edited before it was published in 1922.

5) An author's letters are often very _well written_, so readers _enjoy_ the style. Nowadays, fewer people write letters, so there are fewer _good_ collections. If you're studying a _classic text_ from the past, then reading the _author's letters_ is a great way to find out about the _context_ (P.45).

6) Some _fiction_ authors use letters to tell the _story_ — see P.99 on letter writing technique.

Travel Writing is a Popular Style of Writing

The Grimmel brothers travelled the world in seach of paradise

1) Travel writing tries to give a sense of what it _feels like_ to be in a particular country — even if you've never been there.

2) There are _loads_ of books and articles written about _travelling_. Many _newspapers_ have a travel section.

2) Some travel books are _guidebooks_ — they're written to tell you _what to do_ when you travel to a country and what to _avoid_, like the _Lonely Planet_ series.

3) Other travel books are written to _describe_ what it is _like_ to visit a place. This includes describing the _culture_, the _lifestyle_ and the _people_. Look out for how much _detail_ is given.

4) These books are usually written from the point of view of an _outsider_. The _native_ culture is described by _comparing_ it with the culture which the _author_ comes from. Bill Bryson's _Notes from a Small Island_, describes travelling around _Britain_ from the point of view of an _American_.

5) Travel books are often _comic_ — they show the _clash_ of cultures between the author and the country he is in. Different cultures _behave_ in different ways (see Section Nine).

6) Some travel books are _well-researched_ by experts; others are written by _first time_ visitors.

Critical Books can help you look at Texts

1) Critical books include books written about _authors_, _actors_ or _politicians_ that look at their _work_ rather than their lives — _The Violent Effigy_ by John Carey is about _Dickens'_ imagination.

2) Critical books are also written by _scientists_, _philosophers_ and _lawyers_.

3) They are written for _two reasons_: to put forward a _theory_ or to attack someone else's theory.

4) A theory is an _opinion_ based on _research_ and _evidence_, which is used to explain facts or events: for example, Einstein's _Theory of Relativity_, or Darwin's _Theory of the Origin of Species_.

5) _Good_ critical books are written to help people to _understand_ — that's why they're useful.

Travel writing on boats is fun — unless it's stormy...

All of these book styles are _non-fiction_. That doesn't stop you writing about them in your _Coursework_ though. Remember — you will _always_ write better about things you're _interested_ in.

Pictures, Posters and Leaflets

You may not think these topics have much to do with English — but you may have to look at a _leaflet_ or a _poster_ when you read an _advertising_ text, and that means you need to know about looking at _pictures_. Otherwise you won't pick up all the _marks_.

Looking at Pictures — Finding a Meaning

Woo haa!

1) Pictures include _paintings_, _photographs_, _sketches_ and _cartoons_ — as well as moving pictures on _TV_ or _Film_.

2) Pictures are attempts to _capture_ what the eye sees — they can be _realistic_, like a photograph or some paintings, or _unrealistic_, like many modern paintings, or cartoons.

3) They use _colour_, _light_ and _shadow_ to create effects of _tone_ — all pictures try to make you _feel_ something.

4) For your _Coursework_ and _Exams_, the most important thing you need to know is how pictures are used _with text_ — for example in _newspapers_ or on _television_.

5) Think about how the picture makes you _feel_ — remember, someone has _created_ the picture to _make_ you look at the world in a certain way. You need to be able to say what that is.

6) See if there is any _text_ with the picture — whether it helps _explain_ the picture, like a newspaper _cartoon_, or the picture explains the text, like a _photo_ in a _news_ article.

7) Think about _why_ the picture has been included — whether it is _relevant_ to the text or not, or whether it creates _bias_: eg An article about government ministers _wasting money_ might have a picture of a minister drinking _champagne_ at New Year. The picture _isn't_ directly relevant to the story, but it gives the _impression_ that _all_ government ministers drink champagne _all the time_.

> Remember — all pictures are biased, even photographs. They create a view of what the world is like using different tricks like lighting and colour.

Posters and Leaflets are Advertising Texts

Bruce McTuce

Live in the Hoose

8.00 pm Sat 25th

1) Posters and leaflets use _pictures_ and _words_ to _advertise_ something. This can be anything from a rock band's tour to a shop sale or a soft drink.

2) A poster is a sheet of paper fixed to a _wall_ or a _board_. It usually has a _small_ amount of text and a _picture_ to catch the eye.

3) The text of a poster will be _brief_ — it's written to give all the important information as _quickly_ as possible. This is like a _slogan_ — advertisers want you to _remember_ their product later. In the case of a _play_ or a _concert_, they want you to remember _when_ and _where_ it is happening.

4) Sometimes the poster will have a _slogan_ or a _joke_: eg "He's back. And this time he's hungry."

5) The picture on a poster will be _eye-catching_ — a photograph of the band looking cool, or a cartoon-style picture. Some posters use _colour_, others use _black and white_.

6) Leaflets are _similar_ to posters, except they are _handed out_ to people.

7) The _problem_ with leaflets is making people _read_ them.

8) They need to explain _what_ they are promoting _clearly_ and in more _detail_ than a poster. They also need to be _eye-catching_ and clear.

9) Look at _where_ the information is given — whether a _free gift_ is offered, or whether the _price_ only appears in _small print_ at the bottom.

Get health insurance today!

10) Look for _dates_, _times_ and any other _information_ on the leaflet.

Advertising with pictures — how to make Monet...

You must learn this page to help you look at _newspaper_ or _magazine articles_, and at _advertisements_. Remember that pictures are _biased_ — even photos can be _altered_ by computer.

Unseen Texts in the Exam

Now it's time to look at the kind of non-fiction _questions_ you'll have to answer in an _Exam_.

Unseen Texts are set as Comprehension Exercises

Pete's method of scanning the text was a little unorthodox

1) Even though you won't see the text until you are doing the Exam, _don't panic_ — you can do _six things_ to improve your chances.
2) You can _practise_ the _skills_ you'll need on any non-fiction text you've never read before. Practise _reading_ and _summarising_ newspaper articles. Write a paragraph on the _style_ and the _tone_.
3) Work out what _kind_ of text it is — a _magazine_, a _newspaper_ or a _travel book;_ a _feature article_ or a _critical text_.
4) The _key skills_ for looking at a text are given in Section Four. Remember to _scan_ the text, read it _closely_, take _notes_ of the important details and be prepared to _answer questions_.

Six Useful Points to Learn

1) _Read_ the questions _carefully_ to decide _what_ the Examiner is asking you to _look for_.
2) _Check_ your _notes_ and then the _text_ to find the answer. If you _quote_ the exact words in the text, make sure you don't forget to use _quotation marks_.
3) _Always check_ to see how many _marks_ are given for each question. _Never_ make your answers longer than they _need_ to be — that's just _wasting time_.
4) Use _all_ the information you're given. If there's a _picture_, make sure you _talk_ about it in any essay question — _why_ it is there, what _effect_ it has.
5) Look for any information _with_ the article or in the _introduction_ which tells you the _date_ and the _source_ of the piece, or even the _author_ — this will help you work out the _context_.
6) See if the passage is an _extract_ from a longer text — this may mean that some parts of the argument are _left out_. Only write about the text which is _actually given_ in the paper.

> Look out for the top five tricks — especially any confusion between fact and opinion. Always remember to read carefully to see if the text is biased.

Comparing and Contrasting is a Popular Exam Question

1) Many _Exam_ unseen exercises will ask you to _compare and contrast_ two or three texts — you will definitely have to do this as part of your _Coursework_ too.
2) The secret is not to panic — _scan_ and _read_ each text _in turn_. Then make a _list_ of what the texts have in _common_, and then what the _main differences_ are.
3) The texts will be about the same _subject_ from different _points of view_.
4) _Context_ will really help you here — if you can say something about the context of each text, it will help you give an _opinion_ on _why_ the two texts have different views: eg a _man_ in _1890_ will have a different view on the _rights of women_ from a _woman_ writing in _1970_, because they come from different _contexts_ (see PP.45-46).
5) Common topics for unseen exercises are: the _Environment, Men_ and _Women_ and _Food_ and _Drink_. They sound boring, but if you _learn_ the skills on this page, you'll get _high marks_ anyway.

> _WARNING:_ don't _attack_ the opinions in an unseen text unless you can give _reasons_. Remember: you _may not_ have the _whole argument_ in front of you.

My favourite unseen text — The Invisible Man...

Phew! Talk about details... but they're all important. You need to know _exactly_ what you are doing when you get into the _Exam_ — that means learning the key skills _now_, so get going.

Revision Summary for Section Six

Lots to revise here. Make sure that everything in this Section is clear before you start Section Seven on Essay Writing Skills. Remember that non-fiction texts don't just contain facts — they also give opinions. You need to read them carefully to see how the style and tone of the piece show the bias of the writer. Go over Section Four on Comprehension Skills — unless you can use them well, you'll struggle with reading any text. Look at the questions below to help you revise what you've covered here. If you have any problems, then go back to the relevant page and look over it again.

1) What is meant by "the media"?
2) What should you look for in non-fiction texts?
3) What are the top five tricks used to create bias in non-fiction texts?
4) Why is information exaggerated?
5) Is non-fiction necessarily fact?
6) Why do you need to be careful with facts and opinions?
7) Is the news fact, opinion or both?
8) What are the differences between tabloids and broadsheets?
9) Give four features of tabloid style. Write a mock article in the style of a tabloid.
10) Give three differences between newspapers and magazines.
11) Where are adverts sometimes hidden?
12) Are statistics reliable?
13) Give two ways that statistics can mislead.
14) What are slogans?
15) What do advertising slogans have in common with poetic texts?
16) How can advertising influence people in negative ways?
17) Give four differences between TV and film.
18) What elements create tone in TV and films?
19) Why are autobiographies popular?
20) How are autobiographies biased?
21) What is the style of a diary like?
22) Why can it be useful to read an author's collected letters?
23) In what way are travel books comic?
24) How can critical books help you?
25) Why is it important to be able to analyse pictures?
26) Give two reasons why a picture might be included with a text.
27) What's the difference between leaflets and posters?
28) Why do you need to look at the layout of a poster or leaflet?
29) What shouldn't you do when tackling an unseen question?
30) What are the six things you can do to improve your chances?
31) What's the secret of comparing and contrasting texts?
32) Why is context important when comparing and contrasting texts?
33) Write a short essay about a TV news programme you watched recently. How was the news presented? Did you spot any of the top five tricks being used? Was the programme giving facts or opinions or a mixture of the two? Did you believe what the programme said?
34) Find a magazine advert and write some notes on how it is written. What is it trying to advertise? Does it use a joke or a slogan? Does it use a picture? Why does it use that particular picture? What style is it aiming for — is it for men or women, young people or old? Would you buy the product because of the advert?

How to Write an Essay

An essay is an attempt to _answer_ a _question_ — it's a short piece of writing on a particular subject. You'll have to write _essays_ for your _Coursework_ and in your _Exams_. This Section is about _how_ to write a _good_ essay, and the common essay _mistakes_ to avoid.

Your Essay Work will always begin with a Question

1) GCSE essays are about _answering questions_ — there are _two_ main kinds you will come across during your English course.

2) _Literary_ essays are essays about specific _texts_ that you have read. You'll have to _respond_ to the text — you must show you have _read_ the text, and _use_ it to answer questions and _give opinions_ about it.

3) _Personal_ essays are essays about a specific _topic_ — like the _Death Penalty_ or the growth of the _Internet_ — where you have to give your _personal opinion_ on the topic, giving _reasons_ to support what you say.

Essays are about Giving Answers

My big mistake was not going to ballet school

1) The biggest _mistake_ that most people make with essays is _failing_ to _answer_ the question. _You mustn't_ fall into this trap.

2) Sometimes the question is given to you _clearly_:

> eg   How do the poems of Owen and Sassoon evoke what life was like in the Trenches?
> What does it mean to be a "gentleman" in _Great Expectations_?
> Does _Twelfth Night_ really have a happy ending?

3) _Read_ the question _carefully_ before you begin your answer. Then give your answer _using_ the _words_ of the _question_, giving _reasons_ and _examples_ to support your argument.

4) Sometimes the question will be _unclear_ — you'll have to work out _what_ it's asking you to do:

> eg   "The problem with Romeo and Juliet is they are too impatient." Discuss.
> Give your opinion on the Environmental policy of this country.
> Give reasons for and against road-building.

5) You need to _rephrase_ these statements _as questions_ — this will tell you _what_ you need to think about, and how to start answering them:

> eg   Are Romeo and Juliet too impatient? Is this a problem?
> What do you think of the Environmental policy of this country?
> What are the reasons for and against road-building?

6) _Be careful_ — the first example is actually asking you to think about _two_ ideas. Examiners often try to _catch people out_ with this kind of question, so keep your _eyes open_.

7) Look at any _extra information_ that's given — if there's a _quotation_, see if the _source_ is given. If the essay question comes at the _end_ of a _comprehension_ exercise, then it'll definitely be _based on_ the extracts given — read them _closely_ and use any _relevant_ information in your answer:

> eg   The example question about Environmental problems would probably come at the end of an exercise about the Environment. You should read the extracts again to find out what information is given about Environmental policy in this country. Then use that information to answer the question, giving your opinion of the policy at the same time.

Essay work — a question of answers...

This is where you really need to _concentrate_ — if your _essay skills_ are good, your _marks_ will be good too. Remember your _reading skills_ from Section Four — if you don't, go over them again.

Coursework Essays

Coursework essays are the _key_ to your written work. If you can write a _good_, _clear_ essay for Coursework, then you'll be halfway to writing _good Exam essays_ too — but you'll need _practice_.

Reading the Question Carefully

1) For Coursework essays, you'll usually be given a _choice_ of questions, either about a _text_ or about a _topic_.
2) _Make sure_ you read through _all_ of the questions. _Don't_ just choose the _first_ one which looks _easy_ — sometimes it may _not_ be as easy as you think. Watch out for _trick_ questions.
3) Take _time_ to work out _exactly_ what each question wants you to do.
4) Look for the _question words_ — _describe_, _explain_, _analyse_, _compare_, _explore_ etc. Each word is asking you to do something _different_.
5) Above all, think what you need to _do_ to get the _marks_ for answering the question.

Essay Questions will ask you What, Why or How

Winston knew all about having two sides

1) _Literary_ questions will ask you about a _text_ or a _group_ of texts. They will focus on what the _themes_ are, what the _characters_ do and _why_, as well as how the text makes the _reader react_ (see Section Five, P.42).
2) _Personal_ essay questions will ask you what the _two sides_ of a _debate_ are (eg _for_ and _against_ something). They'll also ask how _you feel_ about it and _why_ you have that opinion.
3) _Remember_ — most questions will only ask you to do _one_ or _two_ of these things. Make sure you answer the question you've chosen _properly_.

Learn the Meanings of the Eight Great Question Words

analyse	= work out the key features	_examine_	= test something carefully
compare	= work out similarities and differences	_explain_	= make clear (what, how, why)
describe	= say/explain what something is	_explore_	= look at something closely
discuss	= argue for and against	_investigate_	= search for facts and causes

Poor Presentation will lose you Marks

1) Your essay must look _neat_ and _tidy_ so the Examiner can read it.
2) Your _handwriting_ must be _clear_ and _readable_.
3) _Space_ your essay out _neatly_ — write the _title_ at the _top_ and _underline_ it, then leave one line _blank_ underneath it.
4) Remember to write in _paragraphs_ — leave a _gap_ between the _margin_ and the beginning of each paragraph.
5) If you make a _spelling mistake_ or write the _wrong word_, put _brackets_ around it and _cross it out_ neatly with _two lines_ through the word. _Don't scribble_ all over it or use a _whitener_.
6) If you _re-read_ your essay and realise you need to _explain_ something, put an _asterisk_ * at the end of the _sentence_ you need to explain, and write a short explanation in the _margin_. This is the _only_ time you should write in the margin.
7) If you find that you need more than _two_ asterisks on a page, you're _not planning_ the essay properly before you write it. Spend some time revising _planning_ and _drafting_ (P.66).

The Best Essay In The World Ever

    My essays are the best in the world ever because (~~I am an absolute genious~~) I practised*.

*the key skills

Essays are like film stars — they need to look good...

You must learn the _eight great question words_ — they'll help you work out what you're asked.

Planning and Drafting

I know it's boring, but the _secret_ of essay writing really is _good planning_. The stupid thing is that most people _practise_ planning, learn how to do it well and then _forget_ to do it when they write.

Proper Planning will pick up Better Marks

1) Some people say that planning is a waste of time — it is if you want to _throw marks away_. In fact it can _save_ you _time_ and _energy_.
2) Planning means _organising_ your material to help you _answer_ the question.
3) The whole point is to _help_ you to work out the _relevant_ material for your answer, and the _right order_ in which to present it. A good _plan_ will help you write a clearer _essay_ — and that means _more marks_.
4) A _good_ plan will tell you what your _argument_ is and which _examples_ you need to _support_ it — that'll save you _loads_ of time when you write.

Ken's plans were of the evil variety

The Six Steps to Planning a Good Essay

I must think first!

1) Work out _exactly_ what the question is asking you to do — _don't panic_.
2) It _doesn't matter_ if you have _no idea_ what you're going to write. Just _stop_ and _think_ for a moment about how to _answer_ the _exact words_ of the question.
3) Scribble a _rough list_ of everything you think might be relevant. Don't worry about the order yet — but _number_ each point clearly so you can _find_ it later.
4) Look at the _key_ word of the question — _how_, _what_, _why_ or one of the _eight great question words_. Go through your list of _relevant points_ and _choose_ the ones that _answer_ the question. To _compare_, divide your list into _two columns_ — _similarities_ and _differences_.
5) Look at the _whole_ question again. Check that you haven't _missed_ anything. Then decide what _your opinion_ is. Use your points to _support_ your opinion — this will be your _argument_.
6) Draw up a _new_ plan — write the _question_ at the _top_, then your _opinion_. Give your _best_ point as the _first_ piece of evidence to _support_ your opinion. Think of _examples_ to support your first point, then _link_ it to the _next point_ you want to make. You'll need at least _five_ points.

> REMEMBER: if you're not sure what your opinion is, state the arguments for and against. Answer the question by comparing the views on each side.

Drafting means Writing a Rough Version

Drafting means your mistakes aren't written in stone

1) This sounds like a real pain — but if you want to do _well_ in Coursework essays it's _worth doing_. Drafting can _stop_ you from writing a _bad essay_.
2) Once you have your _plan_, you should have your _basic argument_ and your _key points_ and _examples_. Drafting is an _easy way_ to see if your plan _works_.
3) Write a _rough version_ of your essay. Think what you want to say and try to _follow_ the stages of your _plan_. Start by _stating_ your _answer_ to the question and giving a brief _explanation_, then introduce your _key point_.
4) Give _examples_ to support your argument. _Stop_ after you've written a _page_. If you think the essay has gone _wrong_ before then, you should stop _straight away_.
5) Ask yourself if your draft _answers the question_, and if the examples _really_ support your points.
6) Think about whether your opinion is _right_ and whether your _first_ point is really the _best_ point. If you're _not_ sure then write a _new_ plan. It's better to start again _now_ than have to do it later.

Don't be like Clinton — he was a draft-dodger...

Planning and _drafting_ saves you time and effort — _thinking_ before writing means _fewer mistakes_.

Introducing Your Argument

The _hardest_ part of any essay is _beginning_ it. The _first sentence_ has to tell the Examiner that you are answering the question, that you are _organised_ and that your essay _isn't_ going to be _boring_. All that from _one_ sentence — so you'd better start _practising_.

Your Introduction needs to Grab the Attention

1) A good introduction does _two things_ — it states clearly _what_ the essay is _about_ and _how_ you are going to _answer_ the question.
2) Don't _waste_ words — Examiners _don't_ want a whole list of every _book_ you've read, and they _don't_ want a summary of _everything_ you're going to say in the essay. They want you to _get on with it_.
3) That means grabbing their _attention_ and showing them that you _know_ what you're talking about — controlling your _argument_ and your _tone_.

Pete tried to get Clive's attention

How to write a Good Introduction

Let me begin with something my Grandma used to say...

1) Your _opening line_ should try to answer the _question_ you were given. If you can't answer it _straight away_, then say how you are _going_ to answer it in your essay.
2) The _rest_ of the paragraph should make your _best point_ and begin your _argument_, explaining how it is _relevant_ to answering the question.
3) Use the _exact words_ of the question. This shows the Examiner that you've _understood_ the question fully. If the question asks you to look at _two texts_, make sure you mention _both_. If you have to give arguments _for_ and _against_ something, give a summary of the _key point_ on _both_ sides.
4) _End_ the paragraph by _summing up_ what you've said. The _next_ paragraph should _develop_ this point, explaining it further and telling the Examiner what _examples_ you're going to use to _back up_ your argument. Keep your argument _clear_.

Example of an Essay Introduction

Why should we sympathise with Willy Loman in _Death of a Salesman_?

Willy Loman deserves our sympathy because he is a victim of the American way of life. He kills himself so that his family will receive the money from his life insurance policy. He thinks it is the only way he can help the people he loves. All his hopes and dreams are shown to be false — and he believes that this is his own fault.

In fact it is the fault of the society he lives in, which says that making money and following your dream are the things that make you a real man. Willy believes this. When he can't make money as a salesman any more, he decides he is no longer a man, and he will be worth more to his family dead than alive. The great tragedy of the play isn't that Willy loses sight of what is important, but that he never understood what was truly important in the first place: the love of his family.

Looking at this Example

1) The opening sentence gives a _clear answer_ to the question. It sounds _sure_ of itself. The rest of the opening paragraph _explains_ the first point — why Willy is a victim.
2) The _end_ of the first paragraph _links up_ with the beginning of the _next_. The first paragraph explains why Willy is a _victim_ — he believes that his failure to succeed is his _own_ fault.
3) The _second_ paragraph _explains_ that in fact the American way of life is to blame. This _continues_ the argument, but makes a _new point_ — about what the great _tragedy_ of the play really is.
4) The essay can now _move on_ — continuing the _argument_ and trying to _answer_ the question.

Essays are like strangers — they must be introduced...

Writing _introductions_ takes practice — you really must sound _interested_, _organised_ and _clear_.

Your Argument

An argument is the series of _reasons_ you give _explaining_ your answer to the essay question. _Everything_ you put in your essay is part of your argument.

A Good Argument _is about being Clear not Right_

1) English essays have _no right answers_. It doesn't matter what essay question you're given — there's no one _correct_ answer.

2) That means you _don't_ win marks for being _right_ in essays — you win them for making a _good_, _well-supported_ and _clear_ argument.

3) In _literary_ essays the Examiners want you to _show_ them that you've _read_ the texts, that you've _understood_ them and that you can _answer_ questions on them, giving _examples_.

4) In _personal_ essays you need to _show_ that you've _understood_ the question, and answer it giving _examples_ to support your _own_ opinion.

> Do try to be clear Graham!   Hmnahmna

Your Argument must be Logical

I change my mind all the time

1) This just means that your argument must _make sense_.

2) Don't _contradict_ yourself. This means saying one thing and then saying the _opposite_ later on in the essay — the Examiner will just think you're _confused_:

> eg   The sole reason Macbeth kills Duncan is because he persuades himself it is his destiny. He uses the witches' prophecy as an excuse — as though he doesn't have any choice in the matter. This is because he is a weak man — he only murders Duncan when his wife pressurises him.

3) The example says Macbeth _only_ kills Duncan because he thinks it's his _destiny_, and then says he _only_ does it because of his _wife_. This is a _contradiction_ — if _both_ reasons are true then there isn't _one_ sole reason. The passage makes _no sense_, so it would _lose marks_.

4) Keep your argument _logical_ — but don't be afraid to _change_ your mind. If you realise that your argument is _wrong_ halfway through the essay, _don't panic_.

5) Just _add_ a sentence saying that your argument up to that point is _one opinion_, but that there's also _another_. Then _explain_ what's _wrong_ with your first argument, giving _reasons_, and continue the essay with your _new_ argument.

Five Major Mistakes to Avoid

1) In _literary_ essays, don't just tell the _story_ in the text — this is a _waste_ of time and you'll only get _low marks_. You need to _answer_ the question and _argue_ in support of your opinion.

2) Don't _digress_ — stick to the point and _answer_ the question. Don't start talking about _irrelevant_ points or small details. Essays are about _answering questions_ to get the marks.

3) Don't _change_ your argument without explaining _why_ to the Examiner. If you _don't_ explain what you're doing, it'll look like you're _contradicting_ yourself.

4) Don't _generalise_ — you must give _detailed_ examples to back up what you say. If you're writing about a _text_, you must give detailed _references_ to _prove_ your point. Always give _more_ than one example. _Never_ make sweeping statements about an author or a text.

5) Don't give _irrelevant_ or _incorrect_ examples — you'll _lose marks_. You must always explain _why_ you've included an example and _why_ it's relevant to your argument. If it's a _quotation_, make sure you know its _context_ — check that it _really_ means what you think it does.

No correct answers — I knew English wasn't right...

English essays are about _how you argue_ — the secret is _learning the right skills_, not the answers.

SECTION SEVEN — ESSAY WRITING SKILLS

Balancing Your Argument

We're not finished with the skills of good arguing yet — we need to talk about _balancing your argument_: giving the views of _both sides_.

A Balanced Argument Looks at All Sides of the Question

Romeo couldn't marry Juliet because she was moving to Paris

1) Even though there are no _correct_ answers to English essays, there are still lots of _wrong_ answers to _avoid_.
2) Never forget that _your_ opinion is just _one_ point of view — _check_ it in case you've _missed_ an important detail.
3) You need to think about possible _problems_ with your argument — whether it really _makes sense_, or whether there is some vital piece of _evidence_ that you've _ignored_ in your essay plan.
4) _Discuss_ these problems in the course of your _essay_.

How to Write a Balanced Argument

For   Against

1) You must _learn_ to argue _for_ and _against_ your own answer to the question.
2) Look at the question from a _different angle_ — think about whether you're really _answering_ it, and whether there are any arguments _against_ your own opinion.
3) Some essays ask you to give _both sides_ anyway — arguing _for_ and _against_, _comparing_ texts, _discussing_ topics. You need to give a balanced argument in _all_ your essays.
4) This _doesn't_ mean writing a _bad_ argument — and it _doesn't_ mean your _first_ argument is useless. The Examiners want to see that you _realise_ there's more than _one_ view about every topic.

Example of a Balanced Argument

   In the opening scene of _King Lear_, Cordelia and Kent are the characters who love Lear most. They refuse to play his games — when the King asks Cordelia what she will say to win a third of the kingdom, she replies "Nothing". When Lear becomes angry and disinherits her, Kent interrupts his King, telling him he is making a mistake. Kent and Cordelia love Lear, which means they are honest with him, and as a result he rejects them.

   The problem is that because of this love, Kent is banished and Cordelia disinherited. Neither of them trust Goneril and Regan, but their banishment leaves Lear in the power of his cruel daughters. This is a strange sort of love. Furthermore, their honesty is like a rejection to Lear. They are the first people in the play to betray Lear. It is actually their love which begins the tragedy.

Comparing and Contrasting in Essays

1) Some essays ask you to _compare_ texts. Read the question _carefully_ to see if it gives any _hints_. Make a list of _similarities_ and _differences_ between the texts.
2) Each similarity and each difference are _points_ for your essay _plan_. You should make each point and then give _examples_ from _all_ of the texts in turn.
3) _Don't_ write all about _one_ text first and then about the _next_ one — that's _not_ a proper comparison. You need to _show_ that you've read all the texts _closely_, and that you can spot the _links_ between them — you're writing about _themes_ and _style_.
4) Always give _plenty_ of _examples_ for comparisons — the Examiner needs to see the _similarities_.
5) _Comparing_ texts will help you pick up _marks_ in _all_ essays — _even_ if you're not being asked to do it. A _good_ comparison shows the Examiner that you _understand_ the text, and you'll win _marks_ for linking it to your wider reading — but it must be _relevant_ to answering the question.

No more weight problems — a balanced argument...

Learning to write a _balanced argument_ means looking at things from _more than one_ point of view.

Examples and Quotation

To pick up the _marks_, you need to give _examples_ to support your _argument_ — especially in _literary_ essays, where you've got to be able to _quote_ from the text.

Giving Examples in Personal Essays

I said ex-ample not egg sample!

1) It's easy to _forget_ examples where you're giving your _own opinion_ — but unless you give them, your essay _won't_ pick up the _marks_.
2) Think about examples from your _own experience_ — things that happened to you which are _relevant_ to the _question_ and relevant to your _argument_.
3) Think about _books_, _films_ or _articles_ you've read that _support_ what you say. If you can, _quote_ the _exact_ words, otherwise just _explain_ what they said. Any _context_ material may be relevant.
4) Always give the _source_ of your example — the _name_ of the book or newspaper, and the _date_.
5) _Never_ make examples up — you'll _lose marks_ if you are caught. Once you have given your example, make sure you explain _why_ it's _relevant_ to the your _argument_ and to the _question_.

Why You Need to Quote from the Text

1) On the last page we looked at comparisons _between_ texts, but a _good_ essay is also about making comparisons _within_ texts.
2) Your essays need to give _examples_ to prove the _points_ of your argument. They must also show that you've _read_ the text _carefully_ and chosen _relevant_, _accurate_ quotations.
3) That means _every_ time you make a _point_ about a text, you should give a _quotation_. _Never_ put a quotation in just because you know it — it must be _relevant_.

A Quotation is a Phrase taken directly from the Text

1) You must quote _exactly_ what the original text says — if you _aren't_ sure, then put it into your _own words_. You must say _where_ it came from in the text.

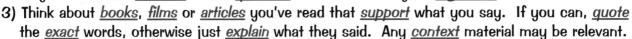

No, Mr Jones, Macbeth did not say, "Is this Mick Jagger I see before me?"

2) Always give a _reference_ for a quotation — for _novels_ give the _title_, the _chapter_ number and the _page_ number; for _poems_ give the _title_ and the _line_ number; for _plays_ give the _title_, the _Act_ number and the _scene_ number. The _first_ time you quote from a particular text in an essay, you should also give the _author's name_.
3) Make sure you explain _who_ is speaking — if it is a _character_, then say so. If it is the _narrator_, then say this in your essay.
4) _Never_ quote _out of context_ — look at the passage _around_ the part you want to quote. _Don't_ use phrases to mean something that they _don't_ in the original — you'll _lose marks_. Check that the phrase _really_ means what you think it does:
   eg The phrase "I loved her," is _out of context_ if the original was "I lied when I said I loved her."

Only Quote Relevant Bits of Text

1) The _secret_ of quoting is choosing _short_, _relevant_ phrases that are easy to _remember_.
2) As you _read_ a text, make a _list_ of key quotations. Note the _page numbers_, to find them again.
3) Keep short quotations as _part_ of your paragraph, and add _quotation marks_ — then give the _reference_ in brackets: eg "Sweet sister, let me live." (_Measure for Measure_, Act III, scene i)
4) Leave the _spelling_ and _punctuation_ exactly the _same_ as they are in the original text.
5) Quotations _longer_ than a whole _line_ should be given as a _separate_ paragraph. Leave plenty of _space_ before and after, and _don't_ use quotation marks.

> ...can be seen in the last lines of the poem:
>
> Better by far that you should forget and smile
> Than that you should remember and be sad.
>   (_"Remember"_, lines 13-14; Christina Rossetti)
>
> The speaker says life should be joyful, even after a loved one dies...

SECTION SEVEN — ESSAY WRITING SKILLS

Essay Style

You must make your essays _interesting_ and _clear_ to read. That means writing _plain English_ so that the Examiner can _understand_ what you're saying and _follow_ your _argument_.

Write Clear Sentences in Paragraphs

1) _Good_ essay style means writing in _proper sentences_ — revise P.32.
2) Vary the _length_ of your sentences — don't just write _short_ sentences or _long_ ones, but a _variety_ of lengths. The important thing is that they're _clear_ to read.
3) Write in _paragraphs_. Every time you introduce a _new point_ or a _different idea_, you must start a new _paragraph_. Don't let your paragraphs get _too_ long or your point will become _unclear_ — break them up with relevant _quotations_.
4) Vary the _tone_ and _vocabulary_ of your essay to keep the Examiner _interested_.

Don't Keep Using the Same Vocabulary

Oo! Ouch! Ouch! Oo! Oo! Ouch! Oo! Oo! Oo!

1) Try to use plenty of _different_ vocabulary in your essays — the Examiner will get very _bored_ if you keep using the _same_ words over again.
2) Make sure you use words _properly_ — if you're not _sure_ about the meaning or spelling of a word then think of _another way_ to say it. Just be _clear_.
3) _Begin_ your sentences in a _variety_ of ways — _don't_ begin every sentence with "The" or "Then".
4) Remember the _two key rules_ for using _adjectives_ and _adverbs_ (see P.21) — you must explain _why_ you've used them. Avoid using words like _"beautiful"_, _"interesting"_ or _"powerful"_ when you talk about texts. You must be _specific_, otherwise the Examiner won't give you the _marks_.

The Tone of an Essay Must be Formal

That Mercutio was bang out of order...

1) Your essay has to _prove_ to the Examiner that you _know_ about the subject and that you can _organise_ material to construct an _argument_.
2) This means you must use _formal language_ — don't forget _grammar_ and _spelling_.
3) You need to be _accurate_ and _clear_ — don't be chatty.
4) Avoid saying "I" this and "I" that — just talk about the _question_, the _text_, the _style_, the _narrator_ or the _characters_ etc. The Examiners _already_ know that the essay is _your_ opinion. _Only_ talk about yourself in _Personal_ Essays.
5) Make sure your _argument_ is _clear_ — if it seems _confusing_ then give a brief _summary_ of what you've said so far, and how it _answers_ the _question_ you were given.
6) _Avoid_ using _clichés_ (see P.2) and _vague_ words, like "nice", "very", "lovely" and "pretty".
7) Watch out for _tautology_ — saying the _same_ thing _twice_ in the same sentence:
   eg   The annual boat race is held every year — _annual_ and _every year_ mean the same thing.
8) Watch your _tenses_: if you _start_ talking about a text or an author in the _past_ tense, you must _stay_ in the _past_ tense. This is _confusing_ — especially when you talk about _characters_ in a text.

Use these Linking Words to Spice Up Your Essay Style

even	moreover	unless	undoubtedly	not only...but also....
despite	however	perhaps	without doubt	possibly
instead	nevertheless	alternatively	even though	furthermore

Essays are like New Labour — a matter of Tone...

Phew! There's a lot to learn on these two pages. If you want to do well in _literary essays_, you must _quote_ from the text. Make sure you know how to do it _properly_. Watch the _style_ of your essays too — silly mistakes will _cost you marks_ even if your argument is clear and well-supported.

Concluding Your Essay

Once you've made _all_ of your points, you need to _close_ your essay and _sum up_ your answer to the question — you must be _focused_.

Summing Up means bringing together the Key Points

1) Start a new _paragraph_ by looking at the original _question_ again.
2) You need to _explain_ to the Examiner how you have _answered_ the question, restating the _main points_ of your argument briefly.
3) Finish by giving a final _example_, or explaining _why_ the question is _important_. Don't go on and on, though. Once you've _summed up_, just write a final _sentence_ as your _conclusion_.

Go Over Your Essay When You've Finished

1) _Read through_ your essay quickly to check that it _makes sense_, and that it says what you _want_ it to say.
2) Check the _grammar_, _spelling_ and _punctuation_. If you find a _mistake_ then cross it out _neatly_ and write the _correction_ above. Don't be _messy_ — you'll _lose marks_.
3) If a sentence isn't _clear_, then cross it out and put an _asterisk_ * beside it. Put another asterisk in the _margin_ beside the sentence, and write what you _meant_ to say in the margin.
4) If a whole _paragraph_ is unclear, you'll have to write the _page_ out again, and rewrite the paragraph so it is _clear_. If the _new_ paragraph means that the _rest_ of your argument is _wrong_, you'll have to write an new _argument_ — only do this if you're _sure_ the argument's wrong.

> REMEMBER: planning your argument properly means that you won't have to rewrite it at the end. Always plan and draft before you start the actual essay.

Don't Panic if You Realise Your Argument is Wrong

1) It's everybody's _nightmare_ that they read through an essay and realise that their answer is _completely wrong_.
2) Sometimes it's not until you actually start _writing_ that you have your _best_ ideas, so your argument should be _flexible_.
3) Don't be afraid to _adapt_ your argument as you go along. Every so often, _stop_ and _read_ what you've written up to that point. If it seems to _answer_ the question then keep going.
4) If it _doesn't_ answer the question then _stop_ writing _immediately_ — work out what the _problems_ with the argument are, then _continue_ your essay, giving the _opposite_ view to what went before.
5) If you realise you've _forgotten_ something really _obvious_ and _easy_, then write a _note_ at the bottom of the _final_ page, _explaining_ what you've done — you'll pick up some _marks_ for _realising_ your mistake. If there's time, write an extra _paragraph_ at the end of your essay, explaining what your answer to the question _should_ have been and _why_.
6) _Never panic_ — you'll have _plenty_ of chances to write _more_ essays for your _Coursework_ folder. Ask if you can _rewrite_ any essays where you made big mistakes — this will help you practise _planning_ your argument and _answering_ the question. _Learn_ from your mistakes.

> Always try to answer the question — even if you haven't got much to say. The Examiners will give you marks for keeping to the point. Never make things up.

Arguments are like gymnastics — you must be flexible...

Keep your conclusions _to the point_, and _check_ your essay so that you don't make _silly mistakes_.

Narrative, Character and Themes

Now we're going to look at how to write _Literary essays_ — how to _write about_ the _features_ of the texts that you've read. Spend some time going over Section Five to help you.

Writing about Narrative means Who and What

1) If you're writing about the _narrative_ of a _text_ or a particular _author_, you need to focus on _who_ is _speaking_ and _what_ they _describe_.

2) Asking who's _speaking_ tells you who the _narrator_ is, and helps you to see the _tone_ and _style_ of the text. _Remember_ that narratives can _change_ their point of view — they can _move_ inside and out of the characters' heads.

> Shirley was suprised by a big hairy monster that said it would eat her up... (tee hee hee)

3) Asking what's being _described_ tells you the _plot_ of the text, and also what the _narrator_ thinks is _important_. If the narrator is in _love_ with a _character_, then the narrative may _only_ talk about _that_ character, nothing else.

4) Look for _hidden meanings_. These can come when the narrator _says_ one thing but _means_ another, or when the _tone_ of the passage makes you feel that the narrator is _wrong_ — eg a passage describes someone being _afraid_ but the narrator seems to _enjoy_ it.

5) These _hidden meanings_ are not stated in the text, but lie _under_ it, so they're called the _subtext_.

> **DON'T FORGET:** look out for opinions being presented as facts in the narrative.

Writing about Characters means Looking for Motives

> But why do you ALL want to borrow my toaster?

1) _All_ characters in texts have _motives_ — _reasons_ why they do what they do.

2) Your _close reading_ of the text should tell you exactly what each character _does_. If you're _asked_ about a character or a group of characters, you need to find _evidence_ in the text which shows you their _motives_.

3) Look at what they _say_, and ask yourself whether they're telling the _truth_. If they're _lying_ then you need to look at _why_.

4) _Remember_ — writing about characters is like a _detective story_. You have to look for _clues_ to answer your essay question.

The Themes of a Text are What It's About

> Runaway train!

1) Concentrate on the _themes_ mentioned in the _question_. All texts have _more_ than one theme but you're only being asked about a _specific topic_. Don't get _sidetracked_.

2) You must give _examples_ from the _whole_ text — look at the _characters_ and the _narrative_.

3) You may want to use _context material_ from _other_ sources — about the author's _life_, or perhaps a _different_ text to _compare_ with the subject of your essay.

4) Make sure your context material is _relevant_ — if it _isn't_, _don't_ use it. You must _relate_ your context material back to the text you're _writing_ about, and back to the _question_.

5) Some authors talk about the _same_ themes in _different_ texts — it can be useful to _compare_ the _views_ presented, but you must show how they're _related_ to each other. This is called _cross-referencing_. All the texts you use must be _relevant_ to the theme you're writing about.

> **Always give examples to support your argument — keep them relevant and accurate, especially any context material you use.**

Treat texts harshly — they'll come apart at the themes...

Here are _three_ of the _most popular areas_ you'll be asked to write essays about. Always be sure that you understand _what_ you have to write about to get the marks — and _how_ to do it.

Writing about Language

You should _always_ try to mention _language_ in your _literary essays_ — even when the _question_ doesn't ask about it _specifically_. The language of a text creates the _style_ and the _tone_.

You Must Write about How a Text Uses Language

Zee new vonder drug vill help you zleep

1) The _language_ of a text is the basic _tool_ for creating _effects_ — look back over Section Five to remind yourself.
2) You need to write about the _vocabulary_ of a text — if it's _simple_ or _complicated_, and if it gives lots of _detail_ or just the _facts_.
3) Comment on any _changes_ in the language between different _parts_ of the text. Write about _why_ the language changes like this — what _effect_ or _feeling_ it creates.
4) Sometimes _characters_ in a text will _speak_ in a certain way — you should ask yourself what this _tells_ you about them. This _trick_ is often used when a character is _poor_ or _foreign_.
5) Sometimes the _narrator_ of a text will _mimic_ the _speech_ of a _character_, in order to comment on what they're saying — perhaps to _mock_ them. This mimicry will be part of the _narrative_ and won't appear in _dialogue_ or _quotation marks_ — see points 6, 7 and 8 in the example below.
6) The _only_ way to spot it is by _reading_ the text carefully to _work out_ how the _characters_ sound when they speak, and how the _narrator_ sounds normally. It takes a lot of _practice_.

An Example of Writing about Language

One of the characters in _Joseph Conrad's_ novel _Lord Jim_, is an _Australian_ called _Chester_, a _dodgy businessman_ who has tried his hand at "anything and everything a man may be at sea, but a pirate." This extract tells us several _important things_ about what he is _like_, just from the _language_ used:

> '"He's been having grub with you in the Malabar last night — so I was told."
> 'I said that it was true, and after remarking that he, too, liked to live well and in style, only that, for the present, he had to be saving of every penny — "none too many for the business! Isn't that so Captain Robinson?" — he squared his shoulders and stroked his dumpy moustache, while the notorious Robinson, coughing at his side, clung more than ever to the handle of the umbrella, and seemed ready to subside passively into a heap of old bones. "You see, the old chap has all the money," whispered Chester, confidentially.'
>
> (_Lord Jim_, Chapter XIV; Joseph Conrad)

1) The scene is _narrated_ by one of the _characters_ involved, because he uses the _first person_ ("I").
2) The _first_ sentence of the extract is spoken by _Chester_ and contains a _grammatical mistake_ — "He's been having" means that the action has taken place over a _long period_ of time, but Chester uses it with _one occasion_: "last night". His _grammar_ tells us that he isn't very _educated_.
3) He uses the _short_ form _"he's"_ instead of _"he has"_, and the _slang_ word for food, _"grub"_. This fits with the fact that he has been a _sailor_ — probably _not_ a very _important_ or _high-ranking_ one.
4) The next sentence is very _long_, and is spoken by the _narrator_. He uses a _varied_ vocabulary and describes Captain Robinson with _clear_, _comic_ image — this means the narrator is _educated_.
5) Chester remarks that he likes to "live well and in style" — he is saying the _same_ thing _twice_ to make it sound more important (_tautology_). He's _showing off_ to the narrator.
6) He then gives an _excuse_ for the fact that he _isn't_ living well and in style — the short clauses "only that," and "for the present," make it _sound_ like an excuse because they _slow_ the sentence down.
7) His excuse is that "he had to be saving of every penny." This is another _grammatical mistake_ — this means that it's in _Chester's_ tone of voice and _not_ the narrator's. The narrator _mimics_ him.
8) Then the narrator _quotes_ Chester directly; "none too many for the business! Isn't that so Captain Robinson?" Chester's _own_ words are used because the narrator doesn't _believe_ this excuse — at the _end_ of the passage, Chester tells us he has no money anyway.
9) _Captain Robinson_ doesn't answer the question, but the narrator _describes_ him looking _ill_. This suggests that Robinson is _weak_, and Chester only wants his _money_ — which he _admits_ at the end.

Writing about Novels

Novels are *long narratives* written in *prose*. Prose is the *opposite* of poetry — writing which *doesn't* have any formal *rhythm* or *pattern*. You'll need to look at *themes*, *style* and *language*.

You Must Write about the Whole Novel

Read the whole thing? You must be kidding!

1) A *good* essay about a novel *moves* between points about the *structure* of the novel as a *whole*, and *detailed points* about specific *passages* in the text.

2) For essays on *more* than one text, *compare* them as *whole novels*, then look at the *details* of specific *passages* as *evidence*.

Writing about the Structure of the Novel

1) Writing about the *structure* of the novel means looking at the *effect* of the *whole* book.

2) Look for the different *kinds* of narrative *voice* — whether there is *one* narrator or *more*, and whether the narrator is a *character* in the book or a *detached observer*.

3) Write about the main *themes* of the book — the *ideas* that keep coming up in different places.

4) You must make *connections* — you need to be able to *link* different parts of the novel which are about the *same* thing. That means you have to *read* the text *closely* and take *good notes*.

5) You also need to make *connections* between *different novels* written by the same *author* — look at the *similarities* and *differences* between the *ideas* in each: whether they *change* or not.

6) Sometimes you may have to *compare* novels by *different* authors — look at the *themes* and the general *style* of the books. *Remember* to make *connections*.

DON'T FORGET: you must give examples to support your arguments about the structure of the novel. Write about specific passages in detail as evidence.

Looking at Passages in Detail

The full stop on page 5 is brilliant...

1) This means using your *comprehension skills* — look at Section Four again.

2) You need to *read* the text *closely* so that you can *explain* exactly what *effects* it creates and what *language* and *tone* are used.

3) You're giving *examples* to illustrate larger points in the *argument*, but you're also showing the Examiner that you've *read* the text and *understood* it.

4) Remember to ask the *six major questions* (see Section Five, PP.43-44). Work out *who* the *narrator* is, and what the *style* of the passage is — for example, a *descriptive*, *narrative* or *dialogue* passage.

5) Look at *how* the novel involves *you* in the action — whether you're told what the characters *think* or you *see* them doing things *without* any explanation.

An Example of Writing about a Specific Passage

It was the last tram. The lank brown horses knew it and shook their bells to the clear night in admonition. The conductor talked with the driver, both nodding often in the green light of the lamp. On the empty seats of the tram were scattered a few coloured tickets. No sound of footsteps came up or down the road. No sound broke the peace of the night save when the lank brown horses rubbed their noses together and shook their bells.

(*Portrait of the Artist as a Young Man*, Chapter Two; James Joyce)

The extract describes the *silent end* of an *evening*. It describes the *emptiness* of the tram and the street. We are told there are *no sounds* in the street except the *horses' bells* shaking which give a *warning* (admonition) that this is the *last* tram.

The *only people* mentioned are the conductor and driver of the tram, who are talking. We *don't hear* what they say, we just *see them* nodding. This adds to the feeling of *silence*.

Writing about Fiction — a novel idea...

Remember — writing about novels means looking at the *big picture* and giving *detailed examples*.

Writing about Plays

Writing about plays doesn't just mean looking at _what_ the _characters say_, but _how_ they say it and what else they _do_ onstage. Plays were written to be _performed_, and your _essays_ must take this into account.

Write about How a Play would look Onstage

1) When you read a play, you need to _imagine_ how it would look _onstage_.
2) Read it _out loud_ or even _act_ the scenes out, using the _stage directions_.
3) Stage directions are any _information_ that appears in _brackets_ which tells you what the characters are _doing_, where they should _move_ and how they should _say_ their lines.
4) You need to look at _what_ the characters say, and _how_ they appear to the _audience_ — characters can _say_ something but _act_ in such a way that we don't _believe_ them.
5) _Remember_ — all the information a play gives about the _characters_ and _story_ must be spoken by the cast _onstage_. The _audience_ watches what happens and makes up their _own mind_ about how the characters appear — whether they're _heroic_, _sympathetic_ or _cruel_ etc.

> _Dialogue_ in a play tells us what the characters _think_ about _themselves_. The way they _speak_ and _behave_ tells us whether they are telling the _truth_ or _lying_.

Plays use Unrealistic Tricks to make a Picture of Reality

1) Plays try to create a picture of the _real world_. This can mean lots of _unrealistic_ things happen, like people speaking _poetry_, _music_ in the background and shifts in _time_ and _place_.
2) Many plays move _backwards and forwards_ in time — like Arthur Miller's _Death of a Salesman_.
3) _Older_ plays, such as _Shakespeare's_ works, tend to follow the story from _beginning_ to _end_. They can cover _long_ periods of time or _short_ periods. Always check the _stage directions_.
4) Often characters _alone_ onstage will speak _directly_ to the audience — the _fancy_ name for this is a _soliloquy_. In these speeches, the character can _explain_ what he or she is _thinking_.
5) _Hamlet_ and _Antony_ (in _Julius Caesar_) have soliloquies explaining what they're going to do. _Iago_ (in _Othello_) and _Richard III_ tell us they're _lying_ to the other characters. Talking directly to the audience _involves_ us in the _plot_ — we _know_ things the characters onstage _don't_ know.
6) Some plays only have _one_ character who tells the _whole_ story — these are called _monologues_: for example _Talking Heads_, by _Alan Bennett_.

Five Key Features to Write About in Plays

1) Look at _how_ the audience is _involved_ in the action — whether _you_ know things that the _characters_ onstage _don't_ know. This can be _comic_ or _tragic_.
2) Think about how the play makes you _feel_ — whether it makes you _happy_, _sad_ or _angry_.
3) Look at the _language_ — whether the play is written in _verse_, or the language sounds _normal_ and _realistic_, or there's a _mixture_ of styles (like in _Shakespeare_). Look at the _imagery_ (P.47).
4) Write about _what_ the characters _say_ and _how_ they _sound_ to you — telling the _truth_ or _lying_.
5) Write about any _performance_ of the play you've seen, including _films_ and _videos_ — how it made you _feel_, and whether you _reacted_ differently when you _saw_ the play from when you _read_ it. _Remember_, any play you see is only _one interpretation_ — the _director_ has read the play and _told_ the actors to perform each scene a certain way (see PP.88-9 on Drama, P.91 on Reviews).

Learn this Note on Quoting Poetry — in Plays and Verse

When you quote poetry, _don't_ just run the lines together like prose. If you quote a sentence where the line _ends_ in the _middle_, draw a _vertical slash_ / to show where _one line ends_ and the next _begins_: "Tomorrow, and tomorrow, and tomorrow/ Creeps in this petty pace from day to day." In most poetry each line begins with a _capital letter_. You must quote it exactly as it is _in the original_.

Writing about Poems

Poetry can be _tricky_ to write about because a _lot_ is said in a _small_ amount of _text_. That means you have to read it _carefully_ — especially for the _language_ and _tone_.

Poetry is about Word Music and Tone

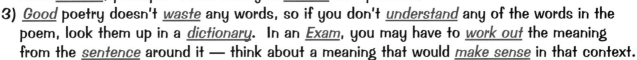

1) _Begin_ by reading the poem _through_. Ask yourself how it makes you _feel_.
2) Look at what the _question_ wants you to _do_ — if it's a _comparison_ or a _comprehension_ exercise then you need to look at _everything_. Sometimes the question may be _specific_ — on the poet's use of _language_, or the main _themes_, perhaps. Make sure you _answer_ the question.
3) _Good_ poetry doesn't _waste_ any words, so if you don't _understand_ any of the words in the poem, look them up in a _dictionary_. In an _Exam_, you may have to _work out_ the meaning from the _sentence_ around it — think about a meaning that would _make sense_ in that context.
4) Look for _hidden meanings_ — sometimes the main _theme_ of the poem _isn't_ mentioned clearly. You need to look at what _happens_ and work out what it _means_ from the _tone_ and the _style_.

> Don't just write about what happens in the poem in your own words. You won't get any marks for that — you have to tell the Examiner what it means.

Older Poems are Easier to Write About

I prefer an older poet

1) You may think that _older_ poems are _harder_ and more boring, but they're also much _easier_ to write about. That means you can win _higher marks_.
2) Older poems often use more _poetic language_ (P.48) and _vivid images_ (P.47).
3) They generally have strong _rhythms_ — so it's much easier to write about the poet's _style_ and use of _language_. See how the _rhymes_ work.
4) The hard part is understanding the _tone_ and some of the _vocabulary_. This comes with _practice_. Remember the _key points_ to look for in older texts (see P.50).
5) _Modern_ poems are _easier_ to understand. This can make it _difficult_ to find much to _say_ about them — if they're very _clear_ then there are no _hidden meanings_ to look for. Just remember to look at the _language_ and the _images_ used. Try to sound _interested_ in what you're writing about.

Writing about the Tone of a Poem

1) The _tone_ of a poem is the _mood_ it creates — it can _change_ between one line and the next. It's formed by the _narrative voice_ of the poem.
2) Read _each_ sentence _carefully_ until you've worked out what it _means_.
3) _Remember_, even though a sentence may be on two or more _lines_ of a poem, it's still a _whole_ sentence that has to _make sense_ by itself.
4) Think about whose _point of view_ the sentence expresses — whether it _does_ make sense, and whether each sentence _follows on_ from the last.

Jim wanted a different point of view

5) Every poem has an _argument_, just like an essay. If the _logic_ of the argument seems _wrong_, there could be a _hidden meaning_ in the poem. If the poem _contradicts_ itself, then this is a deliberate _trick_ by the poet — look out for _contradictions_ and _write_ about them.
6) Poems are about _feeling_ — sometimes the _emotion_ of a poem _affects_ the argument. _Don't forget_ — the feelings expressed in a poem _don't_ have to be _real_. Poetry is a form of _fiction_ — even when a poem talks _directly_ to the reader, it uses a _poetic voice_. It is _not_ the poet talking.

Writing about poetry — going from bad to verse...

Writing about poetry can be tough. Learning the _rules_ on this page will help you to write about _poetic tone_ — that's where most people _lose marks_. See Section Ten for some _revision examples_.

Writing Exam Essays

Exam essays are *not* like *Coursework* essays — you won't have as much *time* and you'll have to make your *argument* as *clear* as possible. If you're *well prepared* there's *no reason* to panic.

How to Prepare for an Exam Essay

1) Some Exam *questions* will be about *texts* you've *studied* during your Course — you'll know what they are *in advance*, so *read* them *properly*, take *notes*, learn *quotations* and *practise* writing *timed* essays.

2) For each Exam, find out *what* you have to *do* and *how long* you'll have to do it. Whenever you *practise*, *time* yourself so that you get *used* to working to a *deadline*. Remember your *comprehension skills* (Section Four).

3) See *how* much you can write within the *time limit*. That will roughly be the *length* of your essay in the *Exam* — make sure you can write a *clear* *argument* and you can *answer* the question *in that time*.

Mervin's only hope was to sweet-talk his teachers

Always Read the Question Carefully

1) In the Exam you *mustn't panic* — read the *whole* Exam paper through *first*. *Don't* just start writing without *thinking*.

2) Then read it through *again* and *mark* the *questions* you think you can do.

3) On a piece of rough paper, *write down* all the *quotations* you've learned. In *some* Exams, you'll be *given* the texts, so don't worry about quotations.

4) Make sure you *read* the *instructions* on the paper *carefully* — especially the *number* of *questions* you have to answer.

5) Work out *exactly* what the question is asking you to *do*. Then *plan* your essay. *Don't* write without a plan — it should only take a *few minutes* to scribble one, and your essay will be *clearer* for the Examiner to follow.

6) Start with your *best point* and begin your answer *straight away*. Don't *waste* time with a *long* and *irrelevant* introduction.

Never Make Any of these Six Mistakes

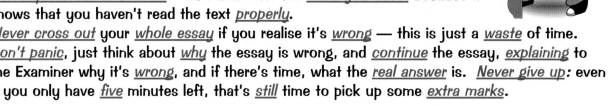
Pam launched straight in without a clue what she was doing

1) *Never invent* things — *don't* invent *examples* or *quotations*. Even if you don't know any examples, you'll *get marks* for trying to *answer* the question.

2) *Don't* get *sidetracked* — *stick to the point* and *answer* the question.

3) *Don't* write without *thinking* or *planning* — a good Exam answer *isn't* about how *much* you write, it's about whether you *answer* the question *clearly*.

4) *Never* learn an *essay plan* in *advance* — it *won't* answer the Exam question you're given, and you'll *lose marks* for an *irrelevant* argument.

5) *Don't quote out of context* — the Examiner will *mark you down* because it shows that you haven't read the text *properly*.

6) *Never cross out* your *whole essay* if you realise it's *wrong* — this is just a *waste* of time. *Don't panic*, just think about *why* the essay is wrong, and *continue* the essay, *explaining* to the Examiner why it's *wrong*, and if there's time, what the *real answer* is. *Never give up:* even if you only have *five* minutes left, that's *still* time to pick up some *extra marks*.

I hate Exams — they're such a testing time...

This is a really important page to learn. Exams terrify people, and that makes them *careless*. The first things they forget are the *basic skills* — reading the *whole paper* through, reading the *question* carefully, *planning* their essay and *timing* it. Just keep *calm* and *answer the question*.

Revision Summary for Section Seven

Another big Section to revise — but don't panic, these questions are here to help. Essay writing is one of the basic skills of English — without it, you'll be lost. Spend some time going over the Section, then look at these questions for some practice. Don't cheat by looking back — see how much you can remember without looking first.

1) What are essays for?
2) What's the biggest mistake that people make in their essays?
3) What should you do when a question doesn't look obvious?
4) What's the most important thing to look at when you read the question?
5) What are the eight great question words?
6) What is each one asking you to do?
7) What should you do if you make a spelling mistake?
8) When are you allowed to write in the margin?
9) If you need more than two asterisks on a page, what's gone wrong, and what should you do about it?
10) What are the six steps to writing a good essay?
11) What should you do if you're not sure what your opinion on the subject is?
12) What should your first point always be?
13) What is drafting? Why bother writing a rough draft?
14) After you've written a page of your draft, what should you do?
15) What does your introduction need to do?
16) What are the four steps to writing a good introduction?
17) What is meant by the argument of an essay?
18) Why must you take care not to contradict yourself in your argument?
19) What are the five big mistakes to avoid?
20) Are there right answers to English essays?
21) Are there wrong answers to English essays?
22) How would you go about writing a balanced argument?
23) How should you compare two texts in an essay?
24) Why do you need to include lots of examples when comparing texts?
25) Do you need to give examples in Personal Essays as well as literary essays/
26) Why do you need to quote from the text?
27) How should you write a quotation that's longer than a whole line?
28) What should you vary in your essays to keep them interesting?
29) Why do you need to be specific and choose the right words/
30) What should the tone of an essay be like?
31) How would you finish your essay?
32) What do you do if you find your essay is completely wrong?
33) What's the key to writing about character?
34) How would you go about writing about the structure of a novel?
35) What evidence should you give when writing about the structure of a whole novel?
36) What are the five key features to write about in plays/
37) Why are older poems easier to write about?
38) How should you prepare for an Exam essay?
39) What are the six big mistakes to avoid in Exam essays?
40) Write an essay on the advantages and disadvantages of school. Remember to plan your essay and give examples to support your points.

Personal Writing

Personal writing means any written work which is about _yourself_ and your _opinion_. It can also include any _fictional stories_ you write, or _real-life experiences_ you write about, as well as your opinions. For personal _essay_ work you should also learn the _Essay Writing Skills_ in Section Seven.

Personal Writing Must Always be Clear

1) When you give your own opinions, you still have to be _clear_. That means your _punctuation_, _spelling_ and _grammar_ must be _correct_. Go over anything you're _unsure_ about in Section Three.

2) Personal writing can be _tested_ in lots of different forms — we're going to look at the most _common_ ones in this Section. The _secret_ of good personal writing is knowing your _audience_.

You Have to Write in the Right Style

I was very concerned

1) You need to choose the _appropriate style_ to use for every piece you write — that means _looking carefully_ at what the _question_ asks you to do.

2) If you asked to write about an _experience_ you have had, then you should use a fairly _formal_ style, but you should also write about your _feelings_ — what it was _like_ to be in that situation.

3) If you're asked to write a _letter_, ask yourself whether it should be _formal_ or _informal_ — for example, if you're writing a letter to a _character_ in a _play_ as a _friend_, you should write an _informal_ letter; if you're writing to the _editor_ of a _newspaper_ you should write _formally_.

4) Some personal writing questions ask you to _imagine_ you're in _contact_ with a _character_ from a _book_ or a _play_, or to imagine yourself in the same _situation_. You need to think about _how_ the characters _talk_, and try to write in a _similar style_.

5) Sometimes you may be asked to write a _different ending_ to a _novel_, or to write a _short story_ with the same _characters_. This means you need to know about the _style_ of the _original_ book, and try to write in a _similar way_. The Examiner will give you _marks_ based on how _well_ you write in that _style_ as well as for how _relevant_ and _interesting_ your story is.

> Choosing the right style means knowing your audience — using the right vocabulary, explaining difficult ideas clearly and keeping people's attention.

Five Elements of Style to Watch Out For

I'm just too cool

That's your opinion!

1) LANGUAGE : make sure your readers _understand_ what you're writing about — especially if you're describing something _technical_, like _sport_ or a _hobby_.

2) VOCABULARY : use a _variety_ of words and don't _repeat_ yourself if you can avoid it — make sure you use new vocabulary _correctly_.

3) TONE : keep the reader _interested_ by varying the _tone_ of your writing — try using some _fiction_ and _non-fiction_ techniques (see next page).

4) HUMOUR : be careful with _jokes_ — they're a _good_ way to keep people reading, but think about whether they'll _offend_ anyone. If they're _not_ funny to the Examiner, you could _lose_ marks — so _think_ before you make a joke.

5) OPINION : if you give an _opinion_ you should try to _support_ it, even in a _descriptive_ essay. The Examiner doesn't just want to know _how_ you _felt_, but _why_ you felt that way too. Try to _explain_ it clearly.

Personal writing — a lonely hearts ad, perhaps...

Personal writing sounds easy — it's only writing about yourself. Unfortunately, that's why most people do it _badly_ and throw away lots of _easy marks_. You have to write your _personal pieces_ just as carefully as _your essays_. Learn the _five elements of style_ off by heart.

Rhetoric

Rhetoric means _persuasive language_ — the way you use words to _argue_ a case, especially _exaggerated_ language. It's a key skill in _personal writing_ — you can also use it in _essays_ too but you must be careful _not_ to say things if there's no _evidence_ to back them up.

You Can Persuade People Using Rhetoric

Ace products will change your life completely!

1) Rhetoric is one of the main _tricks_ used in _fiction_ and _non-fiction_ texts to cause a _reaction_ (revise the top five tricks on P.53).

2) You can use it in your writing to _argue a point_, or to encourage a _reaction_ in the reader.   It will show your _opinion_ — your _bias_.

3) You can also use it in _public speaking_ — in _debates_ or _speeches_. _Politicians_ and _journalists_ use rhetoric to make their points _sound_ more _important_ than they really are.

4) One trick is to exaggerate _feelings_ when you describe them: for example, _journalists_ will say things like "His career is _finished_," or "This result is the _end of the world_ for Welsh football." They don't literally _mean_ this — they're using _over-the-top_ language to make the reader _react_.

5) Another _trick_ is to use lots of _questions_ without giving the _answers_. This invites your reader to _accept_ what you say and _agree_ with you, as though they couldn't _possibly_ disagree.

6) You can also _repeat_ words and phrases to _emphasise_ them for the reader.

7) You can also _attack_ the _opposite_ view to your own, by making _jokes_ about how _wrong_ they are, or by finding an _extreme example_ of that view in order to _outrage_ your audience.

8) _Good_ rhetoric will often give a _slogan_ — or _soundbite_ — which is easy to _remember_ and makes a _key point_. It can _encourage_ people to _do_ something.

9) One of the _cleverest_ tricks is to _identify_ yourself with your audience — when you write about _your_ reactions use "_we_" and "_us_". This encourages the _audience_ to _agree_ with _your_ view.

Two Examples of Writing Using Rhetoric

Look _closely_ at these texts — see how many _rhetorical tricks_ you can spot in them.

We have all heard what the Environmental protesters say. They're concerned that more roads means the destruction of more of the countryside, and the destruction of more plant and animal life. These are the same protesters who walk out in front of drivers on busy motorways, causing terrible accidents, risking their own safety and the safety of other people. These are the same protesters who talk about their concern for life. That doesn't sound much of a concern for life, does it? If they were really concerned about life they wouldn't endanger the lives of innocent drivers, would they?

The road builders talk about reducing the amount of traffic in towns by building roads in the countryside. They talk about reducing exhaust emissions into the air of our towns for the sake of our children. They seem to ignore the fact that it was their roads which caused these problems in the first place. Can't they see that building more roads is not a solution? In ten years time they'll still have to build more. It's time to take a stand, to stop the road builders and ask the government to look for a real and permanent solution — improving public transport and reducing the number of cars on the road by raising taxes. Let's be cruel to our wallets to be kind to the planet.

Rhetorical language — I don't believe it...

Rhetoric is a really useful trick to practise for your personal writing. Remember — it's about _persuading_ the Examiner to _agree_ with you — and to give you _high marks_ for your writing.

Writing about Experiences

Writing about _experiences_ means trying to put down on paper a particular _moment_ in your life when you felt a certain _feeling_, or something specific _happened_ to you.

Answer the Question You're Given

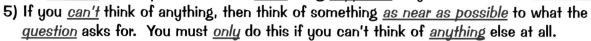

She's a great listener.

1) Most _experience_ pieces come with some sort of _guideline question_: for example, *Write about a time when you were jealous.*

2) These questions could come up as _Coursework pieces_ after you've been reading a _text_ in class, or part of a _comprehension exercise_ in your _Exam_.

3) Start by _looking_ at any _texts_ you were given — for _ideas_ about what you have to _describe_, and the _feelings_ you need to _capture_ in your writing.

Write about your best friend.

4) Think about _your_ experiences and try to come up with one where you _felt_ the _emotion_ in the question, or the _same_ thing _happened_ to you.

5) If you _can't_ think of anything, then think of something _as near as possible_ to what the _question_ asks for. You must _only_ do this if you can't think of _anything_ else at all.

6) _Start_ your piece by explaining _why_ your experience is _relevant_ to the _question_: for example, "I remember the first time I was jealous of my brother."

7) If your experience isn't _exactly_ the same then _say_ so _immediately_, but _explain_ why your experience is _similar_ and _relevant_: for example, "Although I have never really been jealous, I used to worry a lot about trusting my cousin, which was similar in some ways."

REMEMBER: you must make your experience relevant to the question — and interesting for the Examiner to read. Think about the tone and the style.

Good Style and Tone will Win You High Marks

All of a sudden, there was water everywhere

1) Even though this is a _personal_ piece, the _style_ of your writing is a _major factor_ in how good a _mark_ you get.

2) You need to make the experience _come alive_ for the Examiner — that means describing it _accurately_ and _interestingly_.

3) It also means _varying_ the _style_ — the _length_ of _sentences_ you use, putting in _dialogue_ as well as _description_ and using lots of _different vocabulary_.

4) You'll need to _vary_ the _tone_ — use the text to make the Examiner _feel_ what you _felt_, make it _funny_, _sad_ or _frightening_.

Start off by Grabbing the Examiner's Attention

1) You need to make an _immediate impression_ on the Examiner — showing that you're writing a _relevant answer_ to the question, and making your piece sound _interesting_ so the Examiner keeps reading.

2) This sounds _tricky_, especially if you think the experience is _boring_ but you can't think of anything else. _Don't panic_ — the _style_ and _tone_ you use can make even a _boring_ piece sound _interesting_.

3) _Don't_ tell the Examiner _everything_ about the experience _right away_ — just give a _hint_ to show that it's _relevant_ to the question and to make the Examiner _want_ to read on: for example, "My first experience of jealousy left me with five stitches and a broken heart."

4) You need to make the Examiner ask the question _"why?"_ If they're _curious_, they'll _want_ to read on to see _what happens_ in the piece.

Personal writing — it can be a fun experience...

If you _learn_ the main points on these pages, you can really _improve_ your _personal writing marks_.

SECTION EIGHT — PERSONAL WRITING SKILLS

Descriptive Writing

After _grabbing_ the Examiner's _attention_, you need to _keep_ it — this means _varying_ your _style_ and _tone_, especially in your _descriptive_ writing.

Descriptive Writing means _Saying What's Going On_

It smells of sprouts

1) _Good_ descriptive writing makes a scene _come to life_ — it _doesn't_ mean you have to describe _everything_ you can think about.
2) You need to give the Examiner _enough_ information to _explain_ what is _happening_ and who is _involved_, but keep your story _moving_ too.
3) You should also try to _set the scene_ — you could describe the _weather_, the _light_, the _colour_ of things, _smells_ and _sounds_.
4) You must try to describe your _feelings_ — this is what the piece is _about_. It's not just _what_ happened, but how it made you _feel_. The piece _isn't_ just a _report_ of the facts — it's also about your _opinion_ of them.

You Can Give _Two Sorts_ of _Opinion_

1) You can describe your _opinion_ at the time — what it was _like_ to be there, how you _felt_, whether you were _afraid_ or _excited_. Try to _imagine_ yourself _back_ in the same situation:

> I hid from the fisherman in the grass by the river. The ground was cold and wet and my t-shirt was soon soaking. I was so scared I couldn't breathe. Then I saw him. He was coming towards me, red-faced with anger. I didn't dare make a sound, but I could hear my heart beating louder. I was sure that if the fisherman came any closer, he would hear it too...

2) You can describe your opinion _now_, looking _back_ at the experience — whether you're _embarrassed_ at what you did or _glad_ that you did it, and what you _learned_ from it:

> Looking back, I still feel a tingle of fright when I think about that fisherman with his knife. Anything could have happened. At the same time, I'm proud that I threw the fish back. It was such a big, powerful thing in the water, with its fins flashing silver-yellow as it swam. I couldn't let it die helpless, flapping desperately on a riverbank before ending up on that smug fisherman's dinner plate.

Practise Descriptions _Using Your Senses_

1) The _key_ to description is using your _senses_. Think about the _sounds_ you hear, the things you _see_, what things are like to _touch_ and _taste_, and how they _smell_.
2) Use these _senses_ to write a _paragraph_ describing the _room_ you're in _right now_. Try to describe as _many_ things as you can. _Don't_ repeat yourself.
3) You should also try to use _comparisons_ — look at P.47 on _imagery_. Try to think of your _own_ images instead of ones you've _read_ in books. _Never_ use clichés (P.2).
4) Remember your _adjectives_ and _adverbs_ — use them to _express_ how things made you _feel_: for example, "He was a beautiful, sleek, black cat."
5) _Don't_ overuse words like "beautiful" or "interesting" in your writing — you must explain _why_ the things you're describing were beautiful or interesting. _Never_ use the word "nice" — it doesn't _mean_ anything. Think of adjectives that give a _clear picture_ of what you're describing.

Good jokes — I can't possibly describe them...

You'll definitely _pick up marks_ for writing about your experiences if you can _describe_ them clearly. Don't forget your _adjectives_ and _comparisons_, and practise descriptions using the _five senses_.

More on Descriptive Writing

Descriptive writing is also about how you use _language_ to create _mood_ and _tone_ — making the _atmosphere_ of your experience _come to life_.

Adjectives and Images Can Affect the Mood

Who turned the lights out?

1) If you want to write about a _happy_ experience then you should choose the right kind of _language_. Use images of _colours_ and _brightness_, or _spring_ and _summer_. You can also describe _happy events_ — _parties_ and _celebrations_, for example.
2) If you're writing about a _depressing_ experience, then use images of _cold_ and _darkness_. Any images of _loneliness_ will also help to create the right _tone_.

Three Ways of Describing People

1) Describe their _features_ — the _shape_ of their _head_ and their _nose_; the _colour_ of their _skin_; the _shape_ and _size_ of their _body_; whether they are _good-looking_ or _ugly_; even their _clothes_.
2) Describe the way they _act_ — how they _walk_ and _talk_; whether they seem _confident_, _friendly_ and _charming_, or _cold_ and _cruel_; whether they have any _annoying habits_ like running a hand through their hair or picking their nose etc.
3) Use an _image_ to describe them — think of something that they _remind_ you of: a _busy_ man could be like a _steam engine_; a _fat_ man _exercising_ could be bouncing like a giant _beach ball_.

Images can be funny or serious, and it takes practice to think of them. The secret is using your imagination — and reading different styles of text.

Use Sentence Structure and Language to Create Tone

1) If you want to create a tone of _suspense_, use _short_, _sharp_ sentences which just explain _one fact_ at a time — try to _delay_ any explanation as _long_ as possible (like _The X Files_). _Don't_ give too much information away. The Examiner will _keep reading_ to see what happens:

> The moonlit field was strangely quiet. Suddenly the light disappeared, blocked by a shadow. The field went dark for an instant. An owl hooted like a ghost. Inside the farmhouse, the sleeping girl shivered. The front door creaked. She woke with a start and looked about her. The house was silent. She lay down again, relieved.
>
> Creak, went the stair. She opened one eye. Creak, creak. She jumped out and hid behind the bed. Clump went the landing. Clump clump. She shivered again, this time in fear. The door began to open and she screamed. "What's wrong, Mary?" said her father.

2) The example above describes something _boring_ — Mary's _father_ coming home to see his daughter — but it _delays revealing this_ until the _end_ of the passage, making the story _exciting_.
3) It _sets the scene_ in the _style_ of a _horror_ story, which makes the reader _think_ that they _know_ what's going to happen — that someone is going to _attack_ Mary.
4) This means the reader is _surprised_. Good _suspense_ writing should try to _surprise_ the reader — be careful not to give any _clues_ away, but make sure that the surprise _makes sense_.
5) _Practise_ this technique — describe something _one way_ when it's actually something _different_.

Keep the Examiner reading — without bribery...

More important techniques for you to _learn_ — but you must _practise_ using them. Start by writing _descriptions_ of two people you know. Try to make one description _funny_ and the other one _serious_. Then write a quick paragraph about your _last birthday_ — in the style of a _detective story_.

Writing Dialogue

Dialogue is any part of the text which is actually _spoken_ by one of the _characters_ in it. You can use it as a _change_ from _descriptive_ writing — letting the characters _speak_ for themselves.

Dialogue Must Be Presented Clearly

1) Every time a _new character_ speaks you should start a _new line_.
2) You must use _double quotation marks_ to show where the speech _begins_ and _ends_. Remember the _rules_ for quotation marks (see P.29).
3) Try to make your dialogue _dramatic_ to read by _varying_ it — you can _split_ a sentence in two in order to _delay_ a revelation:

"The murderer," said Holmes, "was you, Watson!" _is more dramatic than_
"The murderer was you, Watson!" said Holmes.

DON'T use the word "said" all the time — think of other words like "answered", "replied", "asked", "wondered", "complained", "shouted", "moaned" etc.

Dialogue Should be Realistic and Create Character

No cwubs up my sweeves for this twick

1) Any dialogue you write has to _sound_ like _real speech_.
2) When you're writing about a _person_, think about the _way_ they speak — if there are certain _phrases_ they use all the time, or they have a _problem_ like a _stammer_ or a _lisp_.
3) Try to _use_ these _features_ when you write dialogue for that person — this will _bring them to life_ and can sometimes be very _funny:_ "Thereth a problem," whispered June. "I've got a lithp."
4) In dialogue you can use _clichés_ and _jargon_ to show the Examiner the way that a character speaks — but _don't_ use them in your _descriptive_ writing _at all_.
5) When you _read_ texts, _look_ at the way that the _characters_ speak — if their speech is written in an _interesting_ or _clever_ way, try using it for the dialogue of one of _your_ characters.

For example, in Richard Sheridan's play _The Rivals_ there is a character called Mrs Malaprop who is very famous for muddling her words. This means she often says one thing when she means something else — "He is the very pineapple of politeness" (Act III, scene ii) when she means pinnacle. Muddling words in this way is called malapropism, after the character.

You Can Use Dialogue to Comment on What Happens

1) Dialogue can be used to give a character's _opinion_ — to let them _comment_ on what happens.
2) This means you have to _put yourself_ into the _mind_ of the character — _imagine_ what they _think_ as well as how they _speak_. If a character is a _farmer_, think about what _kind_ of things a farmer would talk about — like the _weather_, the price of sheep etc.
3) Keep the comments _relevant_ to the rest of the piece — if you write about being _rescued_ by a _lifeboat_, you could have a _lifeboat man_ saying, "That was a lucky escape!"

Realistic dialogue — the talk of the town...

Any dialogue you write must sound _realistic_ and give some idea of what the _speaker_ is like. Think about _how old_ they are and _what kind_ of _words_ they would use — they should say what they _feel_.

Writing Stories

Some people find this incredibly _hard_ — they can never think of anything _interesting_ to write about. _Don't panic_ though — writing stories means using the _same techniques_ you use for writing about your _experiences_.

Stories Use _Descriptive Writing_ **and** _Dialogue_ _too_

1) _Good news_ — this Section has _already_ covered _most_ of the _key techniques_ you need for writing _stories_.
2) There's one _big difference_, though — in a story you _don't_ have to write about something that _really happened_.
3) This means you can use your _imagination_ — which can be _great_, but it can also be _difficult_ if you can't think of anything.
4) The _secret_ to story writing is finding a _good plot_.

Finding a _Plot_ **and** _Using it to Write_

All feared the lethal hands of Brucela Leeoni

1) Plots are the _basic outlines_ of what _happens_ in a story.
2) You'll need to decide on a _plot_ and the _characters_ — this will help you decide how _long_ the story is going to be before you start.
3) _Lots_ of people write _bad_ stories because they choose a _plot_ which takes _too long_ to write, so they get _bored_ and _end_ the story _quickly_. You'll _lose marks_ for this, because the Examiner will see that you've _rushed_ the _ending_.
4) You _don't_ have to be _original_. There's no such thing as an _original_ story. _Every_ story you know in _books_ or _films_ is based on something else — often a _mixture_ of different stories.
5) Look at some stories you _like_ — think about the _main events_ that happen. Then think about the _characters_ and try to _change_ them. You could write a story like a James Bond _adventure_ with a girl as the main character, or a _horror_ story about a statue coming to life.
6) Don't just copy — you'll lose _lots of marks_ if the Examiner can see that you've _copied_ the story of a film without _changing_ it in any way. You need to take the _outline_ of the plot and then write your _own story_, in your _own style_ to win yourself high marks.

Choose a _Simple Plot_ **and** _Write the Story_ _Your Way_

That's half-time and only one side in it... Over to you Des

1) When _choosing_ a plot, think about how _long_ your piece needs to be, and how much _time_ you've got to write it. Don't try to write an _entire novel_.
2) Think about the _style_ of the piece — you could write in the style of a _news report_, or give a _football commentary_ on a battle between two alien spaceships. Make sure you keep to the _same style_ — _don't change_ style unless you make it _clear_ to the Examiner.
3) You must use the right kind of _language_ for the _style_ you choose. If it's a _news report_ then it should _sound_ like one — the same is true whether it's a _horror_ story or an _adventure_.
4) Think about the _atmosphere_ you want to create — how you want the Examiner to _feel_ reading the story. Use the techniques of _descriptive language_ and _dialogue_ to create the _tone_ of the story and to bring the _characters_ to life (revise the last four pages if you're unsure).
5) Use you _own experiences_ if you can't think of anything else — you can _change_ the _names_ and the _details_. This can help you to write about the characters' _feelings_.

Guy Fawkes liked stories — he loved a good plot...

You can use your _descriptive writing_ and _dialogue_ skills for writing _stories_ too — with the _right plot_.

More on Story Writing

Here are several more _important points_ to consider when you write stories. _Remember_ — writing _good stories_ takes just as much _effort_ and _practice_ as writing _good essays_.

Choose a Voice for Your Narrator

1) Your story has to have a _narrator_ — someone to _tell_ the tale.
2) You need to _decide_ if the narrator is a _character_ in the story.
3) If the narrator is a _character_, then write as if you _are_ that character — this is a _first person narrative_, using _"I"_ and _"we"_.
4) A first person narrative is like a _personal experience_ piece. You'll need to talk about how _you felt_ at the time, and give _your opinion_ on what happens. Look over the last four pages to remind yourself of the skills you'll need to use.

He knew he had only five minutes to make it to the two for one kipper sale

5) Alternatively, you can use a _third person narrative_. This means describing the characters as _"he"_ and _"they"_. You'll need to write about what _they think_ and _feel_, not just what _happens_.
6) _Remember_ — once you've _chosen_ a narrator, you must _stay_ in the _same_ voice. _Don't change_ the _style_ of writing or the Examiner will think you've _forgotten_ who the narrator is.

Start in the Middle and then Set the Scene

1) The _best_ stories start right in the _middle_ of the _action_ — they make you want to _read on_.
2) You need to be _direct_ — you can use _dialogue_ to do this: _"Don't jump!" shouted the soldier._
3) _Don't_ start off the _same_ way all the time — try to use _different tricks_ in different stories.
4) The _tone_ and _style_ of the story are fixed by your _first sentence_ — you need to let the Examiner know that you're in _control_ of the story and you're _deliberately_ writing in a _certain style_ to create a particular _tone_.
5) Give the Examiner the _key information_ to work out what's going on. That doesn't mean _explaining everything_, but you must explain _enough_ so that it's _clear_ what is happening.
6) You could _set the scene_ by inventing a _source_ for the story.

> The cover of the book seemed ordinary enough, but inside was the most beautiful story I had ever read. It began like this...

What to Put In and What to Leave Out

1) You _can't_ describe absolutely _everything_ that happens. That means you must keep your descriptions _relevant_ to the story as a whole.
2) Think about the _outline_ of your story — and _focus_ on what's going to happen next.
3) Ask yourself what the Examiner _needs_ to know to _understand_ the story, and what's _irrelevant_.
4) Think about the _style_ of your piece. If it's in the style of a _travel_ piece, then you can add _lots_ of _description_ and _detail_. If it's a _detective_ story then _don't_ give _too much_ description — you don't want to _give away_ any _clues_ as to who the _murderer_ really is.

End Your Story Properly — Before You Run Out of Ideas

1) _Plan_ the _end_ of your story _before_ you start writing — this _outline_ will help you decide which information is _relevant_ or _irrelevant_ for your _descriptions_ and _dialogue_.
2) Don't get _sidetracked_ and forget your _plot_ — you'll _lose marks_ if the Examiner can't _follow_ the story because you're busy describing things. You'll _lose marks_ if you don't describe _anything_.
3) You must _tie up_ the whole plot at the _end_ — don't leave anything _hanging_. _Never_ end a story by saying, "Then I woke up — it had all been a dream." Examiners _hate_ that ending.

A sad autobiography — the story of my life, I suppose...

Beginning and _ending_ properly will win you marks. _Don't_ just make your story up as you go along.

Writing Drama

The Syllabuses allow you to write some _personal_ pieces of Coursework as _drama_. Be careful, though — this isn't as _easy_ as it sounds. The Examiners will be _extra strict_ when they mark a piece of drama.

__Drama Writing Must Have a _Clear Purpose___

Unrealistic? This? I should be so lucky

1) You may be given a _question_ which asks you to write a piece of _drama_ on a _subject_, or to write a _new scene_ using _characters_ from a _well-known_ play.
2) _Don't worry_ — you _don't_ have to write an _entire_ play. The Examiners want to see _what you know_ about drama, and whether you can _write_ a _dramatic scene_.
3) Drama is about writing _good dialogue_ so that when it's _spoken onstage_, the _audience_ will _believe_ in the characters and the scene.
4) Drama can be _realistic_ or _unrealistic_ — see P.76.

> The characters of a piece of drama are the fictional people who appear onstage; actors are real people who pretend to be the characters. Don't confuse them.

__How to _Write a Drama Script___

1) The _script_ is made up of the _dialogue_ and the _stage directions_. Stage directions are _notes_ written in _brackets_, telling the actors _how_ to _perform_ the play. They're _not spoken_ at all.
2) All plays are divided into _Acts_, which contain _scenes_ — a scene is a _short_ piece of _continuous action_. Whenever the play _moves on_ in time, the scene _changes_. An _Act_ is a _major_ division between different _sections_ of the play. Stage directions give the _Act_ and _scene numbers_.
3) Stage directions _set the scene_ — they tell the reader _where_ and _when_ the scene happens and _who_ is involved. They can give brief _description_ of any _costumes_ or _props_ a character needs.
4) Stage directions explain _who_ comes _onstage_ and _when_ they do it. They can also say _how_ the person is supposed to _behave_ — _angry_, _sad_, _drunk_ etc — and how they should _say_ their _lines_.
5) The stage directions must be _relevant_ to the scene. You write them to tell the actors _what_ to _do_, where to _move_ and how to _behave_. Don't put in any _irrelevant_ information.

__The _Dialogue_ Tells the _Story___

I'm leaving you Colin, you'll never see me again

1) In a piece of drama, the _only_ information which the _audience_ are given is what they _see_ and _hear_ onstage.
2) The _dialogue_ and the _acting_ must tell the _story_ and create the _characters_.
3) _Think_ about how each character _speaks_ — how _old_ they are, what kind of _language_ they use and what _mood_ they're in.
4) Work out _how many_ characters appear in the scene, and what each one is _like_ — you need to use the _dialogue_ to bring them _to life_.
5) _Vary_ the _emotions_ of the characters — for example, make one _happy_ and the other _sad_. During the course of a _scene_ the characters' emotions may _change_, _reacting_ to what happens.
6) Make the dialogue _interesting_ — ordinary conversations can be very _boring_. Try writing an _argument_ scene, or a scene when someone is told some _bad news_. Remember, the characters need to _react_ to anything which is said.
7) Think about the _style_ of the piece — if you're writing about _characters_ from a _famous_ play, _don't_ change their personalities. Try to write in the _same style_ as the original. Examiners could use these questions to _test_ how well you've _read_ the text.

__My Mother wanted me on the Stage — leaving town...__

Writing dramatic scenes is an _optional_ exercise, but if you do it _well_ you can pick up _lots of marks_. Thinking about _stage directions_ and _dialogue_ will also help you to improve your _play-reading skills_.

More on Writing Drama

Now you need to *learn* about *how to present* your drama scene and *bring it to life*.

Laying Out a Drama Scene

1) Start by writing the *Title* of the piece, and the *Act* and *scene* number. If you're just writing a *scene* on its *own*, then call it *Scene One*.

2) Then write the *stage directions* — begin with *where* the action happens and *when*, then describe *who* is onstage at the *start* as well as any *props* which need to be there (like a table or a bed).

3) *Remember* the *rules* about what information needs to go in the *stage directions* — but don't *waste time* putting in *irrelevant* details.

4) Make sure it's *clear* to the Examiner what's *going on*. You must imagine that you're writing for the scene to be *performed* — give a direction for when the *theatre lights* should come on.

5) Then write the *name* of the first character to *speak*, and then the first piece of *dialogue*. Each time a *new* character speaks, write their *name* on a *new line* and then add the dialogue.

6) Whenever a character needs to *do* something in the scene, put in a *stage direction*. You can write this in the *middle* of the dialogue, so that the *actor* will do it at the right *time*.

7) If a *new* character enters you need to give a *cue* — this means a *stage direction* which tells them *when* to come *onstage*. If a character *leaves* the stage, they also need to have a *cue*.

8) When the scene is *finished*, you must write a *final* stage direction saying what any character *left onstage* should be *doing* as the *lights* fade. When the lights fade, write "End of Scene".

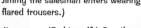

> The Greatest Play
> In The World Ever
> Act One
>
> Scene One
>
> (Leeds, 1975, a bed superstore, there are some beds. The lights come on as Jimmy the salesman enters wearing flared trousers.)
>
> Jimmy: (To himself.) Oo, these beds are marvellous.

An Example of a Drama Piece

The Card Game Scene One

(*The story takes place in California during the Klondike Gold Rush. Mickey is sitting at a round table dealing cards to himself. He is a big man who laughs a lot. Beside him is Josh. Josh is a small, sinister man dressed in black. Every few minutes he coughs into a big handkerchief. Lights up.*)

Mickey -   It's gonna be a fine game! He won't know what's hit him!

Josh -   Shut up and keep practising. (*He coughs into his handkerchief. Mickey looks up at him*)

Mickey -   Say... You ought to see a Doctor about that cough.

Josh -   (*wheezing from the effort of coughing*) After the game... (*He coughs again*).
   (*Enter Walker. He is a smartly dressed man with a small moustache*)

Walker -   Coughing again Mr Hamilton? You really should see a Doctor. Good evening , Mr O'Brien.
   Tell me, are you ready to lose more of your money tonight?

Josh -   (*under his breath*) Not this time!

Walker -   I beg your pardon?

Mickey -   He said "Like last time."

Think about How it Would Look Onstage

1) *Make sure* that you *think* about how the play would appear *onstage*. *Don't* just have characters *sitting around* — give them things to *do*, make them *move around* the stage.

2) *Remember* that the *dialogue* should sound like *real speech*. Try saying it *to yourself* until it sounds *natural*. Don't *forget* that you can use *rhetoric*, though. Look back at P.81. See if you can bring the scene *to life* with an *argument*, or one character *persuading* another.

Writing Drama — getting your act together...

Learn the rules for *presenting* drama — look at the example too. Think how it would look *onstage*.

Writing Responses to Texts

These _writing exercises_ are very _popular_ with Examiners at the moment. You have to _read_ a text and then _write_ about it as if you _were_ one of the _characters_, or as if you were giving them _advice_.

Writing as a Character from a Text

1) The _secret_ of this exercise is _imagining_ what it's _like_ to be the character.
2) You need to think about what the _character_ is like — how they _speak_, how they _act_, what kind of _language_ they use, whether they're _good_ or _unpleasant_ people.
3) The _only_ way to find these things out is to _read_ the text _carefully_ (see Section Five).
4) These features will help you decide what the character's _point of view_ is.
5) When you've _decided_ this, you must _answer_ any question in the way that you think the _character_ would. You should also try to use the same _style_ of _speaking_.

Giving Advice to a Character from a Text

1) You need to choose the _right style_ for your answer — _read_ the question _carefully_.
2) It should _tell_ you _who_ you are supposed to be and what _style_ to write in.
3) Who you are will tell you what _relationship_ you have to the character — whether you're a _friend_ or a _relative_ and can therefore write _informally_; or whether you're a _journalist_ or a _police officer_ and have to remain _formal_.
4) You could be asked to write several _different styles_ of answer — _letters_, _diary entries_, _news reports_ etc. _Make sure_ you write in the _style_ you're supposed to.
5) Think about the _language_ you use — the _tone_ and _style_ of it. If you're writing a _newspaper report_, think about how _journalists_ write (see P.92). If you use the _right style_ then you'll pick up plenty of _marks_.
6) Remember to _answer_ the question — _only_ give advice about the things you're _asked_ to: for example, if you're asked to write to _Juliet_ to advise her to _stop_ seeing _Romeo_, _don't_ give her advice on the best _new music_ in the shops.

Use your imagination — talk about the characters as though they're real people. The more imaginative you are at bringing texts to life, the more marks you'll win.

Writing an Additional Piece for a Text

To be, or not to be, by Jimminy

1) This is a much _less common_ exercise but it's still an _important_ one to _practise_.
2) You may be asked to write _another scene_ for a _play_, or a _passage_ from a _novel_.
3) This means you have to look at the _characters_ and the _style_ of the text.
4) You're trying to make _your_ piece as _similar_ as possible to the _original_.
5) _Never_ invent things as a _joke_ — don't put _alien invaders_ in a scene from _Shakespeare_. The Examiner _won't_ find it as _funny_ as you do.

Writing as a Play Director

1) The _director_ of a play is the person who brings the text _to life_ for a _performance_. The director _interprets_ the play and _decides_ how the actors should _move_ and _speak_ onstage.
2) A popular _Exam question_ is to ask you how _you_ would _direct_ a scene from a play. This means you need to explain _where_ you would have the actors _standing_, _how_ they would _behave_, and what kind of _emotion_ they would use when they said their _lines_. You'll need to _practise_ this.

Give advice to characters — go on, be an Agony Aunt...

Writing in response to texts means _careful reading_ first, and using your _imagination_ in your answer.

Writing Reviews

A _review_ is a _short essay_ which tells you what a _book_, _film_ or _theatre performance_ was like. It should talk about the _themes_ and the _presentation_ and give an _opinion_ on the whole thing.

Start a Review with a Brief Description

1) The _first step_ in a review is to explain _what_ you're _reviewing_.
2) You need to _explain_ to your reader what the _title_ is and what _kind_ of _book_, _film_ or _play_ it is.
3) For a _theatrical performance_, you should also say _when_ and _where_ you saw it.
4) _Don't_ explain the _entire story_ — just give an _outline_ so that anyone _reading_ the review will understand what you're talking about, even if they _haven't_ seen the film/play, or read the book.

> Last Thursday I saw the new production of Chekhov's _Three Sisters_ at the Strand Theatre in London. The play is about how the lives of three sisters have become trapped by circumstances. They all want to escape from their real lives — they all talk about leaving the small town they live in and going to Moscow — but they are unable to do anything about it. This makes the play very tragic and very funny.

A Theatre Review Tells You About the Performance

1) Writing a _theatre_ review means talking about the _performance_ you saw.
2) Start by making _general comments_ about how the _director_ has chosen to _present_ the play — many old plays by _Jonson_ or _Shakespeare_ are sometimes performed in _modern costumes_.
3) Write about the _set_ — some plays have a _large_ set with lots of _scene changes_, other plays have _no set_ and the actors _mime_ all the props.
4) Look at _costumes_, _music_ and _lighting_. These things are all part of the _experience_ of going to the theatre. _Music_ and _lighting_ can _change_ the way we _feel_ about a _character_ or a _scene_.
5) Write about the _acting_ — whether it was _good_ or _bad_ — particularly if there was a _very good_ performance by _one_ actor. _Remember_ to explain _why_ you thought it was good.
6) Give _opinions_ on how the _performance_ went — whether it was _exciting_ or too _slow_, whether you could _hear_ the actors properly. _Always_ give _reasons_ for your opinions.
7) Finish by _summing up_ the _strengths_ and _weaknesses_ of the performance and give a _final opinion_ on whether you would _recommend_ the production to other people. Ask yourself whether you _believed_ in the _characters_ and the _story_ — if you _didn't_, then explain _why not_.

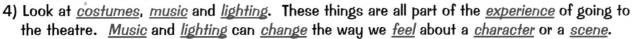

Book and Film Reviews Explain What the Work is Like

1) _Book_ reviews should look at the _style_ of the book and whether it's a _good story_. You should also write about whether it's _easy to read_ or _dull_, and whether or not you _enjoyed_ it. You must give _reasons_ for your opinions, like a short _essay_.
2) _Film_ reviews look at the _style_ and _story_, but they also look at the _acting_, the _music_ and the _images_ of the film — whether it's an _epic_ film with _lots_ of characters and dramatic scenes, or it's a _low budget_ film with a _few_ actors.
3) You can use any _facts_ you know about the _context_ of a book or film in your review. Make sure they're _relevant_ though (to remind yourself what context is, look at PP.45-46).

Carol realised she couldn't afford ANY actors

Book, Film and Theatre reviews — what're they like...

This is definitely something you'll have to do for your Coursework. Remember — _reviews_ are just like short essays. You need to talk about _style_, _tone_ and _language_ — and then give your _opinion_ on whether you liked it or not. Don't forget to give _reasons_ for your opinions, though.

Writing Reports

A report is an _account_ of a particular subject — a _description_ of the _facts_. You may be asked to write reports about _events_ you've been to for your _Coursework_.

A Report Concentrates on the Facts

1) The most _common_ kinds of reports are _news_ reports, _sports_ reports, _weather_ reports, _business_ reports and _government_ reports.
2) The _difference_ between a _report_ and a _review_ is that a review is about giving an _opinion_, a report is about giving the _facts_ of an event or a situation.
3) _Reports_ are also about _description_ — you need to _describe_ what the event or the situation is _like:_ for example, a _business_ report about a proposed new type of _car_ needs to describe _what_ the car would be _like_, and look at the _advantages_ and _disadvantages_ it might have.

Henry took his arts reviews very seriously

Description can bring a Report to Life

1) A _good_ report will give the reader a _feeling_ of what the situation is _like:_ a _news_ reporter tries to give a _sense_ of what it's _like_ to be on the scene — what's _happening_ and _why_.
2) The _secret_ of good reporting is good _descriptive writing_ (see PP.83-84).

Why You Need to Practise Writing Reports

Daily Stuff and Nonsense

Man Gives Birth To Gas Fire Shocker!

Dave Smith, 38, from Hull, said "They thought it was coal from the Ultrasound."

1) You may have to write a report about an _event_ at _school_, or about a _sports match_ that you went to.
2) You may also have to write reports in the _style_ of a _newspaper_ as an exercise in writing _responses_ to texts (see P.90).

How to Write a Good Report

1) _Describe_ the facts _carefully_. Try not to be _biased_ but explain _exactly_ what happened, and if you can, _why_.
2) Describe the _scene_ — think about the _six major questions_ from Section Five (PP.43-44): _what_ happened, _where_ and _when_ it took place, _who_ was involved, _how_ it happened and _why_.
3) If you can _answer_ all these questions you'll write a _clear_ report — make sure it's as _accurate_ as possible by _checking_ it through.

Example of a Sports Report

League-leaders United were deservedly beaten in the cup last night by non-league minnows Beanthwaite Rangers.

Rangers took a shock early lead after two minutes when pacy left-winger Wensley stepped inside his marker and hit a low cross to the front post for striker Daley to tap in.

Things were soon back to normal for United fans though, as former England star David Buckingham was brought down roughly after the restart.

Buckingham got up to score a scorching free kick from just over the half-way line, leaving Rangers' keeper "Big" Little with no chance.

At one-all the game became scrappy, with Rangers' players harrying United into making basic mistakes. No clear opportunities were made by either side, until a stunning forty yard run from Daley brought the winning goal. Ecstatic Beanthwaite boss Chris Digby praised his players: "They were immense. Winners all the way."

Beanthwaite go on to meet cup holders Aspinall in the next round. Meanwhile United will really have to pull themselves together before Wednesday's crucial European tie with Zaron Belgravia. Manager Harrison must be worried.

Writing Letters

Letter writing is a _skill_ you'll need to _practise_ for _everyday life_ as well as for your _Coursework_. There are _two_ main kinds of letter — _formal_ and _informal_ — and _formal_ letters have _strict rules_ of presentation.

Learn these Seven Rules for Formal Letters

1) Write your _name_ and _address_ in the _right-hand corner_ of the page, then _leave_ a line and put the _full date_ underneath — _day_, _month_, _year_.
2) Then write the _name_ and _address_ of the person you're _writing to_ on the _left-hand side_ and leave a line.
3) Underneath this write, "Dear Sir or Madam," if you _don't_ know the person to whom you're writing, or, "Dear Mr..." or "Dear Ms..." with the person's _name_ — eg Dear Ms Jones.   Dear Mr Peters, etc.
4) Then write a sentence explaining _why_ you're writing the letter:
   eg _Re: Application for a Bank Loan_
5) Start the letter using _formal language_ — explain _clearly_ and in _detail_ your _reasons_ for writing.
6) Leave a _line_ of space between each _paragraph_, and _don't_ let the paragraphs become too _long_.
7) _Close_ the letter properly — if you _know_ the person's name write "Yours sincerely"; if you _began_ with "Sir"/"Madam" you must use "Yours faithfully". Print _your name_ then _sign_ above it.

Urgent delivery for you, chief

An Example of a Formal Letter

writer's name and address ⟹ Ivor Drudge
Inland Revenue
Finsbury Road
London
SW7 4GHR

recipient's name and address

William Shakespeare
Anne Hathaway's Cottage
Stratford-upon-Avon

date ⟹ Tuesday 15th November 2005

Dear Mr Shakespeare, ⟸ dear + name

Re: Unpaid tax bills ⟸ subject of letter

introductory paragraph

It has come to our attention that you have not paid any income tax for the past 389 years, despite the sizeable royalties you must be receiving from the success of your plays.

I am hereby notifying you that payment is due within the next month. Please find enclosed a bill for the exact amount owed. Should you fail to pay, the Inland Revenue Office will be forced into legal action. Non-payment is a criminal offence.

I look forward to hearing from you soon,

Yours sincerely, ⟸ correct ending
I Drudge
Ivor Drudge ⟸ print name then signature above it
Tax Inspector

Informal Letters Don't Have Strict Rules

Informal letters are letters to _friends_ and _family_. You _don't_ have to give a _full_ address, just the _date_. Call the person by their _first name_ and use _informal endings_, like "love" or "best wishes".

Look for a letter-writing job — good post to have...

Writing _formal letters_ is easy if you learn the _seven rules_. You may have to write letters in your _Exam_, giving advice to _characters_ from literary texts. Practise writing _formal_ and _informal_ letters.

Presenting Your Work

Presentation is a major factor in picking up _good marks_ — whether in _essay_ work or _personal writing_ pieces. Examiners will give _higher marks_ to _neat_ work which is _easy_ to read.

How to Structure Your Page

1) _Structuring_ your page means using a _clear layout_ so that the Examiner can _read_ your piece _clearly_ and in the _right order_.
2) Start by writing out the _number_ of the _question_ in the _margin_. Then write out the question _in full_, or give the _title_ of the essay or piece.
3) Leave a _blank line_ and begin to _write_ the piece. _Only_ begin writing _after_ you have _planned_ what your _answer_ is first. Most _messy_ pieces of writing are _badly planned_.
4) If you're _not sure_ about your plan then write a _draft version_ of the piece. Then you can _check_ it for _mistakes_ before you write the _final_ version.
5) Try to write as _clearly_ as you can, _without_ rushing. If you _rush_, you're _more_ likely to make _mistakes_ and then you'll have to _cross things out_. You could also _smudge_ the ink by rushing.

Toby put the finishing touches to a perfect essay

REMEMBER: write out neat versions of all the pieces in your final Coursework folder _before_ the deadline. Then you _won't lose_ any marks for presentation.

Avoid Any Grammar, Spelling or Punctuation Errors

: or : ?

1) _Any_ mistakes in these areas will automatically _lose you marks_, no matter how good the content of your written work is.
2) These _errors_ can be _avoided_ if you're _careful_, and if you make sure you know the _rules_ in Section Three. _Learn_ the list of words on P.108.
3) _Practise_ any areas where you _know_ you're _weak_ — the _mistakes_ you make _regularly_. If you _don't_ learn to _avoid_ them, then they could seriously affect your _marks_ — so spend some time _working_ on them _right now_.

Cross Out Mistakes Neatly

1) This is one of the _worst mistakes_ you can make in _presentation_.
2) _Never_ scribble all over a mistake or spend ages crossing it out — because it'll make the page look _messy_ straight away. In fact, the Examiner's attention will be _drawn_ to the _mistake_.
3) When you _cross out_ a mistake, you want the examiner to _ignore it_ and carry on reading what you've written instead.
4) Put _brackets_ around the mistake and draw _two horizontal lines_ through the word or phrase. This will make it _clear_ that you want the Examiner to _ignore_ it. _Don't_ draw _crosses_ over everything.

When brackets just aren't enough...

Read the Instructions for Presentation Tips

1) This is a _stupid_ thing to _lose marks_ for, but people do it every year.
2) _Before_ you begin an Exam, _read the instructions_ carefully to see if they mention _presentation_.
3) Sometimes the _instructions_ will say that you should only write on _one side_ of the paper — if you _don't_ you will _lose marks_. Reading the _instructions_ is part of your Exam too.
4) If _nothing_ is mentioned then you can write on _both_ sides — but make sure you _check_.

Examiners are shallow — they like good-looking work...

Bad presentation can cost you _lots of marks_ — so _structure_ your work and _read the instructions_.

Revision Summary for Section Eight

There's plenty for you to learn in this Section. Personal writing sounds easier than essay work, but in fact it's just as difficult. Make sure you know the skills you need, particularly for descriptive writing and writing about your experiences. Remember — you're trying to bring the experience to life for the Examiner. Never forget to read the instructions you're given, though — that could cost you lots of expensive marks. This set of questions will help you revise the key information from the Section — as long as you read them through carefully before you answer them and follow the instructions exactly.

1) What are the five elements of style you need to use in your personal writing?
2) What is personal writing about?
3) Explain briefly what rhetoric is, and how you can use it: a) in personal writing b) in essays.
4) List four rhetorical tricks and explain how they work, giving an example of each from the two texts on P.81.
5) Why should you vary the style and tone when you write about your experiences?
6) Why do you need to grab the Examiner's attention immediately? How do you do that?
7) What two kinds of opinion can you give in your experience writing?
8) What does descriptive writing do? Give two tricks you can use in descriptions.
9) What are the three ways of describing people? Write three short descriptions of someone you know using each of the three ways in turn.
10) Write a short passage about a dungeon. Try to describe it clearly, giving a sense of what it is like to be there.
11) Write a short passage about a big party, describing it in detail.
12) Write the opening paragraphs of a novel. Try to grab the reader's attention immediately and introduce the story, using description and dialogue. Only give the key information.
13) How do you decide on the plot and style of a story?
14) Write the outline for a plot about a masked bandit helping the poor. Don't just copy a famous story — think of your own version.
15) Write a short first person narrative about a race.
16) Write a short third person narrative about a fight.
17) How should you lay out a drama script? Give a brief example of the opening of a scene.
18) Write a review for the last film you saw.
19) Write a review for the last book you read.
20) Imagine that you live in Ancient Rome. You have just found out that Brutus and Cassius have decided to murder Rome's ruler, Julius Caesar. Write a letter to Caesar warning him about the conspiracy. Remember to address him formally as a ruler, and try to include details that fit the setting — for example, "I will meet you behind the Circus Maximus tonight to give you full details of the plot". Try to make the letter believable — you're playing a role.
21) Write a report for a sports match you saw recently.
22) Write a report on a big news story. Remember to give the facts as clearly as you can.
23) Write a formal letter to a famous living writer, asking them for any tips they have for writing. Remember to follow the rules for formal letter writing.
24) Write an informal letter to a friend telling them about a typical day at school, and what your ideal day would be if you could do anything you wanted.
25) Give five key features of good presentation.
26) Only answer the questions with even numbers in this revision summary. If you've done all of them then you obviously didn't read all the questions through before starting. Don't make the same mistake again.

Talking About Culture

Many of the texts you will read for your English course come from *different cultures* around the world. The *ideas*, *themes* and *images* of the texts come from their *own cultures*.

Every Text is Grounded in a Culture

1) It *doesn't matter* where in the world you are, a text is always *affected* by the *culture* in which it *was written*.
2) The *ideas* and *themes* important to people in *England* have always been the source of literature *in England*. The same goes for *Wales*, *Ireland* and *Scotland*. Even though these countries share the *same* language, their literature can often be very *different*.
3) The same thing is true of *any* literature written in English; whether it comes from *India*, from *Africa*, from *Australia* or the *USA*.
4) The culture *behind* a text is part of its *context* (see P.45).

Early computers were frowned upon in many American states.

English is Spoken all over the World

1) *Many* countries around the world have English as a *native language* or as one of the *official languages* of that country. This *doesn't* mean their *culture* is English.
2) These countries are mostly *former colonies* of the British Empire, now *independent*.
3) This is one of the reasons why English has become the *unofficial language of the world*.
4) The other main reason is the *power*, *wealth* and *influence* of the *USA*, particularly in the *media*.

Countries where English is the official language

Alaska U.S.A.
Canada
United States of America
Hawaiian Islands U.S.A.
Belize
Jamaica.
Dominica
Sierra Leone
Ghana
Nigeria
Uganda
Zambia
Botswana
Zimbabwe
South Africa
Falkland Islands
South Georgia
United Kingdom
Ireland
India
Australia
Tasmania
New Zealand

Be Aware of Other Cultures When You Read Texts

1) Many of the *expectations* of our culture are *irrelevant* to texts from *elsewhere*.
2) Don't *judge* before you *read* them — try to *understand* what it's like to *live* in another culture.
3) *Don't forget* — the *themes* of literature are *similar* all over the world, in *any* language. People will always fall in *love*, make *friends*, *betray* each other, *fight enemies* and try to live their lives in *freedom*.
4) When you read texts from *other* cultures, you must try to *identify* with the *characters*, just as you would with any other text.
5) *Ask* yourself whether there are *similarities* between the *feelings* of characters in the text and feelings *you* may have. The *situations* and *experiences* may be different, but you are a *human* too. Literature is always concerned with *learning* about the experiences of *others*.

What's a D'Urberville?

Cultures — even yeasts have them...

One last topic to go. You'll *definitely* have to look at texts from other cultures during your course — so make sure you learn the *key skills*. Remember — *don't judge* a text before you read it.

Cultural Context

The central skill in this Section is _empathising_. It means reading _without prejudice_, and trying to _identify_ with characters from _cultures_ and _situations_ in which you've never been.

Cultural factors create Identity

1) **LANGUAGE** — Every culture identifies itself by the _language_ it uses. This is why many different cultural _groups_ in Britain today still _keep up_ their _own_ languages and dialects alongside English: for example, _Urdu_, _Hindi_, _Arabic_, _Hebrew_, _Jamaican_, _Welsh_ and _Gaelic_. It's also why different _areas_ of Britain maintain their _dialects_: for example, _Yorkshire_, _Geordie_, _Cockney_, _Scots_ etc. This is very important for literature: the poets _Benjamin Zephaniah_ and _Derek Walcott_ use _Jamaican_ dialect for much of their writing.

'ey up!

I worship flowers

2) **RELIGION** — When you read texts from other cultures you should always look for _clues_ to the _religion_ of that culture. Many religions have sets of _rules_ and _customs_ that people living in that culture have to _obey_: for example, women _dress_ differently in _Islamic_ cultures, and many religions _forbid_ the eating of _pork_.

> **DON'T FORGET:** Many famous texts have been influenced by religious culture and imagery — including Irish texts like the novel _Portrait of the Artist as a Young Man_, by James Joyce, and the poetry of the Welshman Dylan Thomas.

3) **WEATHER** — This may sound strange but the _weather_ of a country does _affect_ its culture. Texts set in _Africa_ or _India_ may be concerned with the problems of _heat_ and _droughts_, or _heavy rains_ during a monsoon season. In the same way, texts set in _Britain_ are often concerned with _rain_...

We like the weather

4) **POLITICS** — Read _carefully_ for any information about _politics_. Many books discuss the _inequalities_ that people face in other countries. _Maya Angelou_ and _Toni Morrison_ write about the political situation faced by _black people_, and particularly by _black women_ in the _USA_. Books like _Cry, the Beloved Country_ (1948) by _Alan Paton_, discuss the racist system of _apartheid_ in South Africa, which existed until very recently. _Chinua Achebe's_ _Things Fall Apart_, is about the impact of _British colonialism_ on the _Nigerian_ Ibo tribe.

I treat _everyone_ the same

5) **GENDER** — This is partly a _political_ issue, but it's also _general reflection_ of different societies, where _women_ are often expected to conform to _traditional ideas_ of _marriage_ and _motherhood_. When you read a text from another culture, look at the way men and women _relate_ to each other. Ask yourself if the women and the men are _treated differently_.

6) **LIFESTYLE** — Different cultures have different _expectations_. In some cultures, everybody must _work_, and education comes second to _survival_. Some cultures in the past were built on _slavery_, and the lives of slaves was _harsh_ and _cruel_. Even though the _main events_ of people's lives are often the same — _birth_, _marriage_, _family_, _death_ — the _culture_ they live will affect what kind of opportunities they have during their lives.

Cultural documents — like theatre tickets I suppose...

It looks pretty daunting, I know, but cultural context is really very easy to spot when you're reading a text. Just look out for these _six factors_, and see if they're _different_ from your culture.

Multicultural Societies

Any text you read has its own _cultural context_ — it doesn't matter who wrote it.

Many Texts are about the Conflicts between Cultures

1) Cultural _conflict_ has become a _major theme_ in modern literature.
2) English is becoming a _world language_ spread by _American_ films, music and culture.
3) Many texts are about the _clash_ between _different_ cultures — particularly in places like _Britain_ where people come from all sorts of _ethnic_ and _cultural_ backgrounds as well as being British.
4) An example is _Farrukh Dhondy's_ collection of short stories, _Come to Mecca_, about the relationship between the traditional _white_ community and the _Bengali_ community in London.
5) Some authors try to bring their two cultures _together_: _Salman Rushdie_ writes about India _and_ Britain.
6) Even in the past, Scots authors like _Walter Scott_ and _Robert Burns_ wrote in standard English _as well as_ Scots, so as to appeal to _larger audiences_.

Robert Burns

Remember the Two Rules of Cultural Context

When you look at texts from other cultures, there are _two rules_ you should always keep in mind:

RULE 1: Think about your own context, and how it affects your understanding of the world, especially your understanding of what is right and wrong.

RULE 2: Look at the context of the text you're reading. Be sure you understand the view of the world presented, and how it's different from your own view.

1) _Don't forget_ to check that you have understood any _new vocabulary_, especially _dialect_ forms.
2) _Always remember_ that English written in other cultures _may not_ follow the same _grammar rules_ as you need for your _Exams_ — read it carefully, but _don't copy it_ when you write.

I knew a stick once — he wanted to dialogue...

Texts from other cultures are specifically mentioned in _all syllabuses_, so you'll certainly have to study them. I know it sounds hard work to find out all about cultural context, but you can pick up a lot of _easy marks_ here if you do your _research_ thoroughly. _Coursework essays_ on texts from other cultures are always _popular_ with Examiners — it means you can do loads of research too.

Revision Summary for Section Nine

Texts from other cultures form an important part of your Syllabus, which is why we've looked at them briefly in this Section. In fact, the skills you need for looking at the texts are exactly the same as for any other. The only difference is the context they were written in, and the context in which you read them.

Make sure you understand the idea of cultural context, and how it affects the way people write. Don't forget that a lot of literature written in English doesn't come from England, and doesn't follow the same rules of grammar and spelling. Just remember that your answers to Exam and Coursework questions must be written in standard English. Try reading some books from other cultures — you could also read translations of books from other languages. All your reading will help your critical skills and improve your writing — which means better marks.

Look over these summary questions quickly, to ensure that you've understood everything in this Section. If you're not clear about something, then go back an look at the relevant page again.

1) Is all literature in English part of the same culture? Explain why not?
2) What is the cultural context of a text?
3) What is your own cultural context? Think about where you live and what your daily life, your family and your friends are like.
4) Give the two reasons why English has become the unofficial language of the world?
5) What shouldn't you do when reading texts from other cultures?
6) Why is it important to look for the similarities between you and the characters in the text, as well as the differences?
7) What are the six factors that create cultural identity?
8) Why is religion important to cultural context?
9) What does the weather have to do with cultural context?
10) What should you think about when you look at gender issues in a text?
11) Why do different groups of people have different dialects?
12) Why is cultural conflict a common theme in literature today?
13) How do authors sometimes try to bring two cultures together?
14) What are the two rules for looking at cultural context?
15) Why is it important to think about your own context when you read a text?
16) Do texts from other cultures always follow the rules of standard English?
17) What should you do if you come across unfamiliar vocabulary in a text?
18) What should you avoid doing in your own work?
19) Write a comparison of your own cultural context with a different context. Try to find five similarities and five differences between the two. What effect do these differences have on life in these cultures?
20) Would you like to live in another culture? If so, then explain why, and which one. If not, then explain why. Make sure you give real reasons, not prejudices.

Looking at a Single Text

Time to _practise_ looking at a few _texts_, using your _comprehension_ and _reading_ skills. Let's start by looking at this famous poem by _William Blake_.

Tyger, Tyger

Tyger! Tyger! burning bright
In the forests of the night,
What immortal hand or eye
Could frame thy fearful symmetry?

In what distant deeps of skies
Burned the fire of thine eyes?
On what wings dare he aspire?
What the hand dare seize the fire?

And what shoulder, and what art,
Could twist the sinews of thy heart?
And when thy heart began to beat,
What dread hand? And what dread feet?

What the hammer? What the chain?
In what furnace was thy brain?
What the anvil? What dread grasp?
Dare its deadly terrors clasp?

When the stars threw down their spears,
And watered heaven with their tears,
Did he smile his work to see?
Did he who made the Lamb make thee?

Tyger! Tyger! burning bright
In the forests of the night,
What immortal hand or eye
Dare frame thy fearful symmetry?

How to Look at this Poem

1) Start by _scanning_ the poem. Then write down what you think it's _about_.
2) Then read the poem again _carefully_. Think about every _sentence_ and every _word_.
3) Now start taking _notes_ — what you think the _theme_ of the poem is and _who_ is speaking.
4) Look at the _style_ — what features of _poetic language_ are used, and what _images_.
5) Look at the _tone_ of the poem — how do the words _sound_? What _tone of voice_ is the speaker using?
6) How does the poem make you _feel_? _How_ has it made you feel this way?
7) Then you can _plan_ your essay. _Remember_ to look for useful passages to _quote_. When you talk about the poem you must give _examples_ to _support_ your _argument_.

A Comprehension Analysis of this Poem

1) The poem starts by describing a _tiger_, but it soon starts talking about an _"immortal"_ creator.
   = _first impression from scanning the text._
2) The _narrator_ of the poem _doesn't_ talk about _himself_, but he gives away something about _his_ character in the course of the poem. He is talking _directly_ to the tiger, _asking_ it questions all the time, _without_ giving or receiving any _answers_ — this means the poem is using _rhetoric_. He's asking _who_ created the tiger and _imagining_ what kind of _being_ or _god_ could have done it.
   = _an opinion on the main theme of the poem based on the general features, and a comment on who the narrator of the poem is. Each point is supported by the text._
3) The poem has a simple _rhyme_ scheme — there are _six stanzas_ (groups of lines) with _four lines_ each. The first _two_ lines _rhyme_ with each other, and the _last_ two lines _rhyme_ with each other. The style of the poem is _rhetorical_, asking lots of _questions_ without answers.
   = _looks at the style of the poem and the features of poetic language it uses._

Looking at a Single Poem II

4) The poem uses lots of *images* of *fire* — in the first line the tiger is *"burning bright"* in a dark forest ("of the night"), in the second stanza the tiger's *eyes* burn and the poet asks who would dare to *seize the fire*, and in the fourth stanza there is a *furnace*.

   There is lots of *physical description* of body parts — belonging to the *tiger* and to the tiger's *creator* — the *"sinews"* of the *tiger's* heart and the *"shoulder"* of the *creator*. In stanza four the poet gives several images of *tools* — *anvils*, *furnaces*, *hammers* and *chains*. This sounds like a description of a *blacksmith's forge*.

   = *looking at the images of the poem and trying to explain what effect they create.*

5) The poem's tone is one of *uncertainty* and *fear* — there are lots of *questions*, but no *answers*, and the *language* is full of words like *"terror"* and *"dread"*.

   = *brief comment on the tone of the poem.*

6) The poem makes you feel *curiosity* and *wonder* — it makes you wonder how a creature as *terrifying* and *beautiful* as a tiger is *created*, and what kind of *being* would create it. It's very *vivid* — especially when it describes the *physical processes* of actually *making* a tiger.

   = *simple note on how the poem made you feel and why.*

An *Example* Extract *from a Comprehension Essay*

The tone of the poem is one of wonder and fear. The narrator never receives any answers to his questions — this creates an air of mystery. It means that the narrator doesn't know the answers, and doesn't know if anything he says is true or not. This makes the poem very uncertain and fearful.

The narrator describes the tiger in a tone of fear — it is "burning" and it has "fearful symmetry." This make him even more afraid of the being who created the tiger — he imagines that the being must be "immortal", and wonders what sort of being would "dare" to create something so terrible and powerful as a tiger.

In stanzas three and four, the narrator imagines what it would be like to make a tiger — how you would physically build one. He imagines the creator twisting the sinews to make the heart, and as he twists them, the heart coming to life and starting to beat. This is a frightening image — the narrator wonders what "dread" (terrible) hands and feet the creator would need.

The word "beat" also has another meaning, to hit, so perhaps the narrator is thinking of the creator beating the tiger's heart into shape. This fits with the next stanza which contains several images of a blacksmith's forge. The word "beat" has two possible meanings, both of which give vivid images of making a tiger.

In stanza four, the narrator imagines that the creator would be like a blacksmith, building the tiger with a hammer and anvil, and making the brain in a furnace. He imagines what it would be like to hold the tiger's claws ("deadly terrors") as you were making them.

In stanza five, the narrator then imagines how the rest of the universe would react to the creation of such a terrible thing as a tiger. He uses an image of personification to give a sense of wonder — the stars throwing down their spears. Then he wonders about the creator himself — whether he was pleased to make something so terrible and "smiled", and whether he could also make something as meek as a Lamb. Here he also means the Lamb as an image of Christian religious belief — the idea that Christ was like a Lamb.

The last stanza is exactly the same as the first, except that the question has a more sinister note. Instead of asking who "could" create a tiger — who was physically able to make one — it asks who would "dare" — what sort of being this creator would have to be.

Comparing Two Texts

The other _key skill_ you need to _practise_ is _comparing_ two texts. _Remember_, everything you say must be _backed up_ by _examples_ — but you're giving your _opinion_.

Read the Two Poems Individually First

Surprised by joy — impatient as the wind
 I turned to share the transport — Oh! with whom
 But thee, deep buried in the silent tomb,
That sport which no vicissitude can find?
Love, faithful love, recalled thee to my mind —
 But how could I forget thee? Through what power,
 Even for the least division of an hour,
Have I been so beguiled as to be blind
To my most grievous loss! — That thought's return
 Was the worst pang that sorrow bore,
Save one, one only, when I stood forlorn,
Knowing my heart's best treasure was no more;
That neither present time, nor years unborn
 Could to my sight that heavenly face restore.
 ("_Surprised by Joy_," William Wordsworth)

Farewell, thou child of my right hand, and joy
 My sin was too much hope of thee, loved boy
Seven years thou wert lent to me, and I thee pay,
Exacted by thy fate, on the just day.
O, could I lose all father now! For why
 Will man lament the state he should envy?
To have so soon 'scaped world's and flesh's rage,
 And, if no other misery, yet age?
Rest in soft peace, and, asked, say here doth lie
 Ben Jonson, his best piece of poetry.
For whose sake, henceforth, all his vows be such
 As what he loves may never like too much.
 ("_On my Son_," Ben Jonson)

Look for the Main Similarities and Differences

Similarities

1) _Both_ poems are about _losing someone_ you love — more exactly, they're both about how it _feels_ to be the person _left alive_.

2) _Both_ poems are _addressed_ to the _dead_ person and both speak about the narrator's great _love_ for the person — _Wordsworth's_ poem calls the person "my heart's best treasure," _Jonson_ calls the person his "best piece of poetry."

3) _Both_ poems recognise that they have _lost_ the loved person _forever_ and that they will _never_ love anything else as _much_ in the future ("years unborn" and "henceforth").

Differences

1) _Wordsworth's_ poem starts with a description of a _particular moment_ when he felt _joy_ instead of _grief_; _Jonson's_ poem begins _immediately_ with his _grief_.

2) _Wordsworth's_ poem starts off with _joy_ but descends into _grief_ as the narrator realises again that his loved one is _gone forever_. _Jonson's_ poem starts off with _grief_ but it is also a _farewell_ — the narrator tries to _come to terms_ with his loss by saying that his son was _lent_ to him, and has now _escaped_ the harsh world and the misery of old age.

Plan your essay based on the similarities and differences — look at the themes, style and tone of the poems to find examples (PP.100-101 will show you how).

Context Information Can Help but Isn't Essential

1) "Surprised by Joy" was first published in _1815_, but in _1812_, Wordsworth's _daughter_ Catherine _died_ — this means the poet had _first-hand experience_ of losing his child.

2) This might mean that the poem is based on a _real-life_ experience — but only "_might_". For a poet like _Wordsworth_, it was important to be true to _feelings_ rather than the simple _facts_.

3) Ben Jonson lived between _1572-1637_, and his _son_ also _died_ very young. Again, he is writing about his _feelings_, but his poem is about one specific moment.

Look for any more similarities and differences between these two poems, then write a practice essay comparing their themes and style. Say which you prefer.

Reading List

Here is a list of books that you should try to read. Some of these books will be part of your Course, others are worth reading anyway because they have good stories. This revision guide has used examples from older texts because these are the ones that cause the most problems. This isn't a complete list, it's just a few suggestions.

Novels

I Know Why The Caged Bird Sings	Maya Angelou
Emma	Jane Austen
Pride and Prejudice	
Mansfield Park	
Captain Corelli's Mandolin	Louis de Bernières
Jane Eyre	Charlotte Brontë
Wuthering Heights	Emily Brontë
Heart of Darkness	Joseph Conrad
The Secret Agent	
A Tale of Two Cities	Charles Dickens
David Copperfield	
Great Expectations	
Daniel Deronda	George Eliot
Silas Marner	
Bridget Jones' Diary	Helen Fielding
The Great Gatsby	F. Scott Fitzgerald
Lord of the Flies	William Golding
The Old Man and the Sea	Ernest Hemmingway
Fever Pitch	Nick Hornby
Brave New World	Aldous Huxley
On the Road	Jack Kerouac
Beloved	Toni Morrison
Jazz	
Animal Farm	George Orwell
Nineteen Eighty-Four	
Anita and Me	Meera Syal

Plays

Waiting for Godot	Samuel Beckett
Popcorn	Ben Elton
All My Sons	Arthur Miller
Death of a Salesman	
The Crucible	
A Midsummer Night's Dream	Shakespeare
As You Like It	
Hamlet	
King Lear	
Macbeth	
Much Ado About Nothing	
Othello	
The Tempest	
Twelfth Night	
Androcles and the Lion	George Bernard Shaw
St Joan	
Arcadia	Tom Stoppard
The Real Inspector Hound	
The Importance of Being Earnest	Oscar Wilde
A Streetcar named Desire	Tennessee Williams

Poetry

Any poetry by W.H. Auden, Elizabeth Barrett Browning, John Betjeman, Robert Browning, Thomas Hardy, John Hegley, Ted Hughes, Rudyard Kipling, Philip Larkin, Louis MacNeice, Wilfred Owen, Christina Rossetti, Siegfried Sassoon, Alfred Lord Tennyson, Derek Walcott, W.B. Yeats or others.

Autobiography

A Postillion Struck by Lightning	Dirk Bogarde
The Diary of Anne Frank	Anne Frank
Unreliable Memoirs I, II, III	Clive James
Bugles and a Tiger	John Masters

Travel Writing

Notes from a Small Island	Bill Bryson
The Kon-Tiki Expedition	Thor Heyerdahl
Blue Highways	William Least-Heat Moon

Remember: anything you read can help your English skills — and marks.

Index

Index

Index

Index

Commonly Misspelled Words

Here is a list of the most common words that people spell wrongly. Learn them now — if you don't you'll just be throwing marks away.

absence	column	grief	occurred	soliloquy
accelerate	commit	grievance	occurrence	sophisticated
acceptable	conceit	handkerchief	omission	souvenir
accommodate	condemn	height	panic	stationary
accurate	conscience	holiday	panicked	stationery
achieve	conscious	humorous	parallel	style
acknowledge	criticism	humour	pastime	succeed
acquaintance	deceive	illegible	permissible	successful
acquire	decision	imaginary	personal	sufficient
across	definitely	immediately	personnel	supersede
address	describe	immensely	philosophy	surprise
aerial	desire	incidentally	physician	suppress
aeroplane	despair	independent	possess	symbol
agreeable	desperate	indispensable	prejudice	syntax
aisle	develop	innocence	preliminary	temporary
amount	disappear	insistent	prescribe	theatre
anxious	disappoint	install	privilege	thief
appalling	disciple	installation	proceed	thieves
appoint	dissatisfy	interruption	profession	thorough
argue	double	irrelevant	psychiatrist	tongue
ask	dread	irritable	psychology	transfer
assistant	eccentric	its	pursue	typical
association	ecstatic	jewellery	quay	tyre
athlete	eerie	judge	questionnaire	umbrella
authorise	efficient	knack	queue	unmistakable
autumn	embarrass	knock	realm	unnecessary
awkward	endeavour	knowledge	reassure	unnoticed
beautiful	exaggerate	labour	receive	until
beige	exceed	laughter	receipt	vague
belief	except	leisure	recommend	vegetable
benefit	excitement	library	relief	vicious
benefited	exercise	likeable	repetition	view
bicycle	existence	loveable	resource	Wednesday
biscuit	extremely	manoeuvre	restaurant	weight
build	fascinate	maintain	rhyme	weird
business	feasible	marriage	rhythm	whole
cease	February	miscellaneous	ridiculous	wilful
ceiling	financial	mischievous	secretary	woollen
changeable	foreign	mortgage	scene	wreath
chaos	forty	murmur	scenery	wreck
cheque	fulfil	necessary	schedule	yacht
chief	fulfilment	neighbour	seize	yeast
chimney	fulfilled	niece	separate	yield
choose	gauge	ninety	similar	zodiac
chose	gorgeous	noticeable	sincere	
college	government	occasionally	skilful	
colourful	grammar	occur	solemn	